One-Anothering

by
Simon Schrock

Calvary Publications

Dedication

To my mother and older brother, who taught me much about One-Anothering (whose pictures are on the front cover),

and

Faith Christian Fellowship, the Church that originally heard these messages, and where we are growing together in these principles.

Copyright © 1986 Simon Schrock

Published by Calvary Publications, Kalona, Iowa

Printed in the United States of America

ISBN 0-940883-00-7

Cover photo by Mary Guengerich
High River, Alberta, Canada

Distributed by Choice Books
11923 Lee Highway, Fairfax, VA 22030   (703) 830-2800

Table of Contents

Preface

THE MODERN SPACE AGE WORLD brings with it much uncertainty and fear. We are caught in a world that honors those flying into space, but can ignore the deep needs of people next door.

Our world honors those who have been to the moon and back, or had a ride through space. But who cares for the person who doesn't make it on the "media blitz"? Who cares for the person who is deeply depressed or in financial trouble? Or caught in a disaster, or feeling of rejection and left out? Isn't there someone to care?

Lawsuits seem to be the order of the day. Neighbors sue each other in order to get their own way. Christian couples go to the judges of the land to receive orders on how to live their lives. The powerful judges direct the lives of many of our children as the parents separate and attempt to settle their differences in court.

The daily lifestyle of the church is too near the same selfish ways of the unchurched. The Washington Post reported that according to a study published for the Princeton Religion Research Center, "morality is losing ground." It cited indications that there is "very little difference in the behaviour of the churched and the unchurched on a wide range of items including lying, cheating, and pilferage."

Is this really the way life should be for a people that are "churched" and considered a Christian nation? Should we be hiring an attorney to beat the other person and make a monetary gain? Should we sue "one-another" in the process of venting our anger and revenge? Should we go to the judge for the directing of our lives?

I believe there is a higher order and calling for the Christian. It is an order that has been tested by time and is reliable for today. It's in the Bible! It's the principle and order of "one-anothering." For the casual reader, it is easy to miss the rich meaning of these short "one-anothering" expressions in the scriptures. The Bible contains concise teachings on what believers should be doing for the other, and what they should not be doing against each other. When these simple and to the point nuggets of truth are taken seriously, it makes a positive difference in our world.

Who will help the fearful, depressed, and rejected? Who will go the second mile in building good human relationships across the line fence? Who will be willing to help carry the load of the other? Who will give directions for the troubled? Who will give hope when hope is gone?

God is calling His people to do that! He calls those who confess His name to be a "one-anothering" people. His people are called to give Biblical directions and assistance to each other.

One-anothering is written with the hope that the people called the church will take these scriptures seriously, live them daily, and become "one-anothering" churches. When this happens, there is renewed hope for our world.

Simon Schrock

Introduction

GOD CREATED US as social beings. Our coming into the world was not an event of our own choosing. Our early survival was entirely dependent on other people who cared about us.

As we grew from total dependency we gradually developed some survival skills. But our overall development was very much conditioned by people around us. Our continued existence is an experience in togetherness.

Simon Schrock has written a book that can enrich the quality of our experience with others at home, at work, and at worship.

We deplore international conflict and terrorism. We are saddened by violence that makes it unsafe to walk the streets of our large cities. The log jam of litigation in our legal system is a further commentary of serious deficiencies in human relations. It speaks of a crying need for "one anothering". Far too often we who are Christian neglect to nurture our relationships with those we know best and love most as we should.

The life of Author Schrock is a testimony that he feels deeply about these things. His theology is intensely practical. His message is easy-reading.

Who can estimate the potential life-changing value of this book? It can begin in me and in you. It deserves a wide reading. May God bless the distribution and effects of this message to the enrichment of people everywhere.

David L. Miller
for Calvary Publications

ONE

Cheer On Your Team

OUR CHILDREN attend the Christian school sponsored by the congregation. On a number of occasions the fathers came to school for lunch with the students and to play ball in the afternoon. The father-son team was a unique arrangement for a good team. When one would hit a 'good one,' there was a lot of 'cheering on'. If it looked like a home run, there was plenty of 'cheering' and 'urging on' to home base. In Bible terms, one could say he was being 'exhorted' on home.

Exhorting means cheering the other on, urging the other to move ahead, to press toward the mark. It means giving encouragement.

The Bible calls believers to encourage one another. 'But encourage one another daily, as long as it is called today, so that none of you may be hardened by sin's deceitfulness.' (Heb. 3:13 NIV)

'Let us not give up meeting together, as some are in the habit of doing, but let us encourage one another—and all the more as you see the day approaching.' (Heb. 10:25 NIV)

It is clear from Scripture that the people of God are to encourage each other. It is not an option; it is a command. God considers giving encouragement so important that He gave some special gifts for giving it. 'We have different gifts, according to the grace given us . . . if it is encouraging, let him encourage.' (Rom. 12:6 & 8) Giving encouragement may be your gift. If it is, you have a extra measure of the ability to encourage others. This does not mean that others need not work on giving encouragement. It is certainly not an excuse for some to be discouraging to others. The Bible command is for all to be encouraging one another.

The Apostle Paul understood encouragement. He used it freely in his opening remarks in his letters to the churches.

To the Corinthians he used these 'cheer on' words: 'I thank my God always on your behalf.'

To the Colossians he wrote, 'We always thank God, the Father of our Lord Jesus Christ, when we pray for you, because we have heard of your faith in Christ Jesus and of the love you have for all the saints.' He encouraged them by affirming their faith.

He urged the Philippians on by saying, 'I thank my God every time I remember you . . . being confident of this, that he who began a good work in you will carry it on to completion until the day of Christ Jesus.' Here he assures them of their worth and value to himself and to Christ.

He praised the Thessalonians for their 'work of faith, and labor of love, and patience of hope.'

One of Paul's 'encouragement principles' can be seen in his greeting to Timothy. In the second letter he first affirms Timothy's faith. He encourages and establishes a kinship. Then he goes on to remind him to 'fan into flame the gift of God.' Notice the principle: he first encourages, then admonishes, then warns, then instructs and teaches for further growth.

Paul used this principle in some correcting and counseling that needed to be given to Philemon. He first acknowledged his strengths. He affirmed him as being a brother. He wrote, 'I always thank my God as I remember you in my prayers, because I hear about your faith in the

Lord Jesus and your love for all saints . . . your love has given me great joy and encouragement, because you, brother, have refreshed the hearts of the saints.' After he recognized his faith, love and strength—after he urged him on, he gave some important counseling. 'I appeal to you for my son Onesimus, who became my son while I was in chains. Formerly he was useless to you, but now he has become useful both to you and to me.'

Much of what is called counseling and correcting among believers is ineffective and hits dead soil. It may not be because the counselor uses the wrong words or gives the wrong answers, but simply that there has been no prior established relationship. There has been no prior affirmation of worth and appreciation for the other person. The counselor has never told him, 'I appreciate you and the way you use your gift for God.' Therefore, the one being counseled has nothing to lose by turning a deaf ear.

If one falls into sin, you may want to admonish that person to return to fellowship with God and the believers. Do you have an acceptance base already established so you can be free to approach him on the matter? Does he have nothing to lose by ignoring your warning and remaining in sin? Practise encouraging others on their strengths, then you'll be in a position to counsel and help nurture growth in their weakness.

How does one encourage another? I'll share six suggestions. First, through words. Check your words; do they make for peace? Do they 'speak things that become sound doctrine?' (Titus 2:1) Do they 'speak . . . truth' with your neighbor? (Eph. 4:29 TEV) Check on your words of the past week. Did they really have an upbeat tempo, the sound of encouragement?

The Christian needs to carefully evaluate his words. Are they 'urge on' words? Sometimes when we are 'just kidding' the other person on his weakness, we may be heaping on discouragement. We do not always know where he may be hurting. What may be kidding to us may be another dose of negative words that further wound his already hurting spirit. Evaluate your words, they may be opposite of encouragement.

Second, couple your words with a firm handshake. When I was a teenager attending church with my parents, the boys would line up outside the church house until just before the services began. Then we would follow the leader to a seat inside. I can still remember this one man would come up the line and give us all a handshake and say our name. I remember how he would shake my hand and say 'Simon.' Way down inside of me, that handshake coupled with my name had an encouraging effect. I felt loved and accepted. Even though he was an older man, I viewed him as a friend. He rated well with me. He practised the Bible teaching to 'greet the friends by name,' and coupled the encouraging word with a firm handshake. (3 John 14)

My mind goes to another older man who has passed into the presence of the Lord. When he shook my hand, I knew he loved me and appreciated seeing me. Encourage another with a firm, affirming, sincere handshake. And just think—there is no name as sweet as their own.

Third, encourage through compassion. Be open and understanding to the hurts of others. Be sincerely sympathetic to their griefs and sorrows. Express sympathy by facing your friend eye-to-eye with words that truly care. My first wife died when I was twenty-five. I was in deep grief. I shall long remember how I felt love and compassion from my own mother when I would visit the home place. One day when I was there, I overheard a remark she made to my older sister. The remark was only a few words, but of deep compassion. Those words are encouraging to me to this day. It was because I felt compassion.

Fourth, encourage through an act. Israel was drawn into battle. The Amalekites attacked Israel. Joshua and his chosen men fought the Amalekites while Moses, Aaron and Hur went to the top of the hill where Moses held up his hands. As long as his hands were up, Israel was winning. When he lowered his hands, the Amalakites were winning. When Moses' hands became too tired, they took a stone and put it under him, then Aaron and Hur each held up a hand of Moses so that his hands were up till sunset. With the act of encouragement, cheering on, holding up the hands of Moses, Joshua won the battle over the Amalakites.

Believers are in many spiritual battles today. They are up against the wiles of the devil. We need to lift up one another with acts that encourage.

Fifth, I've been encouraged many times with a smile from another person. One specific time was at the memorial service of my mother-in-law. My oldest brother gave me a smile as he walked by me to view the body. I understood what it meant. It was encouraging at such a time.

When your pastor preaches the word, give him an approving smile. Let him know you are awake and with it. A sincere smile encourages, but a snooze is downright discouraging. It has been reported that it takes 66 muscles to frown and only 12 to smile. It's easier to smile, it gives encouragement, and it looks better. Smile!

Sixth, encourage through prayer. Think of the unsaved! Appeal to God on their behalf. Through prayer encourage them to yield to God, because it is not God's will that any should perish.

Think of your pastor. Pray that he will speak sound doctrine. Pray that he will have a fresh inspiration from the Lord to share with the flock. Pray for others around you who are having times of testing and struggling with difficult situations. Encourage others by interceding in their behalf through prayer.

Why should we encourage? It's a threefold answer. First, to urge others to come into a right relationship with the Lord Jesus. Believers should encourage unbelievers to take the step of faith by believing on the Lord Jesus Christ and trusting him for their savior and sin-forgiver. Encouragement also means helping others submit to Jesus, willingly allowing Him to be Lord of their lives.

Second reason to encourage: to build up the body of Christ. Within the church members are to encourage others to be 'rooted and grounded in love,' and to be 'builded together for an habitation of God through the Spirit.' We are to be 'cheer leaders' and urge others on in becoming strong in Christ.

Third reason: we are to urge others on to a meaningful life work. We need to affirm the work of one another. Urge others on as they build houses, work in factories, milk cows to feed the world, repair machines to keep commerce moving. Urge others on to help them become successful in being parents, providers and good, honest business people.

Exhort one another! I think of times when others exhorted me. I think of one of my school teachers who saw enough bad in me, and enough good, that she thought I would become a minister some day. That was encouraging.

I think of my Aunt Emma, who spent a good part of her life in a wheelchair. She exhorted me by affirming that she saw 'someone' in her nephew. She expected something from me in the future. Her expectation was encouraging.

Then I think of my editor friends who nutured me along in writing. Eventually the writing resulted in having a book published.

Just think, what kind of church would you have if you really exhorted, encouraged, urged on, cheered on one another. Of course, we cannot do it of our own strength, but from the inner strength available from God's Spirit that dwells in the believer.

Think of the words you used during the past day. Try

to think over the past week. You might be surprised how lacking your conversations are of exhorting words. Try for one week to use only words and comments that are encouraging to those who hear you. Do something different for this whole week—encourage one another!

Believers are the team for God. Urge them on!

TWO

Urge the Other Upward

BUILDING A HOUSE is an accomplishment. I have helped to build houses, and I have helped tear them down. Building a house takes skill, time and work. However, there is a fulfilling sense of satisfaction in building and seeing a finished product. It is rewarding to look at a completed job while the owner calls it a 'great piece of work.'

To tear down and demolish a house doesn't take much skill or workmanship. An inexperienced worker can take a sledge hammer and wrecking bar and make splinters in short order. However, I don't recall receiving compliments of a 'magnificant job' or of 'skillful talent.'

In 1896, Henry Ford completed his first automobile. He put a lot of time, experimenting and work into the project. Later, Ford designed and built the 'Model T.' This was a car the average American could afford. From 1908 to 1927, there were fifteen million sold. Before the 'Model T,' only the wealthy could afford cars. Because of Ford's hard work and simple design, he put America on wheels. Henry Ford built something.

The boy who loves his dog, strokes his fur, gives him a bear hug and teaches him tricks, is doing something constructive and upbuilding. He is developing a friend. The boy who drops his cat from the upstairs window to see if she lands on her feet is being destructive. He is making an enemy.

Believers are to be builders! They are to be constructive. In the Bible, this is called 'edifying one another.'

'Let us therefore follow after the things which make
for peace, and things wherewith one may edify another.'
(Romans 14:19) Another translation says, 'the building up
of one another.' (NAS)

Romans 15:1,2 issues a call for believers to be
builders. 'We who are strong ought to bear with the fail-
ings of the weak, and not to please ourselves. Each of us
should please his neighbor for his good, to build him up.'
(NIV)

To edify means to build up, construct, confirm, to
teach, to improve. To build up mentally or morally.

Believers have been given a serious and important
calling. This responsibility often does not get the attention
it should have. Instead of building each other up, we often
do the opposite and tear each other down. We put the
other persons down in order to be a notch above them.
This is wrong!

God calls for helping the other move upward and
Godward. When I was a boy on the farm, we had a dog
named Fido. He and I were good friends, and I taught him
to do various tricks. One of those was climbing a ladder.
While the ladder was leaning against the hay mow in the
barn, I would tell Fido to 'graddle nuff.' That is the Penn-
sylvania Dutch way of saying 'climb up.' I would get him
started up, then come along behind him. As he nervously
climbed up one rung, I'd 'edify' him on to the next one.
Step by step, I urged Fido on up until he reached the top
and climbed onto the hay ahead of me. This is what God
wants us to do for each other. Step by step, we are to edify
one another upward by building them up and making
them strong.

Edifying means you'll be concerned about getting the
other person up the ladder ahead of you. As you urge the
other up ahead of you, you rise along with him. Can you

imagine what spiritual giants we would become if every-one became 'edifiers.' 'Therefore, encourage one another and build each other up.' (1 Thess. 5:11, NIV)

'Urging Up'

Perhaps the other person's job seems meaningless and her or she is losing interest. When the future looks disgusting, get behind them and affirm their worth and work. Let them know their work is of value and distinc-tion. Don't leave the impression that your job is more important.

If he is a builder, give him your respect. Providing housing is an important job.

If he is a farmer, affirm him in providing food for the world, 'as unto the Lord.'

If the person is a hospital worker, express apprecia-tion for helping the sick and the needy.

If it's a father struggling with his rebellious teen-agers, get behind him with honest caring and understand-ing. Strengthen him to hang in there.

If she is a mother discouraged with the routine, help her see past the little tots messing up the living room to seeing little human beings moving up the ladder into young men and women who become tomorrow's leaders.

My father had an old wooden silo next to the barn. Each fall neighbors got together to 'fill silo.' As the silo filled with load after load of chopped corn being blown in from the top, there was more pressure, or settling, on the bottom. One fall Saturday was silo filling at our farm. On Sunday the pressure of 'settling' began to show. The pres-sure was too much, causing the old silo to begin leaning. It was in danger of falling over. To prevent the pressure from doing its total damage, there was a quick propping up project put into action. The old silo was given support with props around it. It was 'edified' to stay up.

When other persons feel the pressures of life settling

in, will their brothers and sisters 'edify' them? Believers are to put the props up, not knock them down.

I continue to be fascinated at overhearing conversations at public lunch tables. Two people 'chewing over' the boss, discussing the pastor, tearing down co-workers or complaining about decisions. I recall an incident of hearing the pastor 'on the burner' and being torn down in a public place. It was destructive and disgusting. It sounded more like knocking out props than putting them up.

Permissible Isn't Always Upbuilding

The Bible points out that some things are permissible, but they may not be upbuilding. 'All things are lawful for me, but all things edify not.' (1 Corinthians 10:23)

Some things may be lawful to do, but they tear down others.

Some things may be lawful to have, but owning it does not 'build up.'

Anything that does not 'build up' is not in your best interest.

Sometimes people say, 'It's my business what I do,' and others shouldn't concern themselves. That is not true where a group takes edifying one another seriously. That group is interested in the welfare of each other. It does become the business of the other what you do.

Is it really only your business as to the music you listen to, or the kind of books you read, or how you spend your money? It should be another's concern if one's music, reading and spending isn't constructive. God isn't satisfied with our being neutral or simply doing no harm. God wants construction. It isn't so much a question of what's wrong with it, as if it is upbuilding for your life and the life of others.

Conversations Should Build Up!

The conversations we carry on are to build up. The

Bible say, 'Do not let any unwholesome talk come out of your mouths, but only what is helpful for building others up according to their needs, that it may benefit those who listen.' (Ephesians 4:29, NIV)

I have been edified from conversations of others. Particularly do I remember one older man who rode along to Bible School where we taught. It was over an hour's driving time, and at the beginning of the trip someone would ask a question or two, and he could use the rest of the travel time in giving illustrated answers. His conversations were constructive, and the passengers were being 'built up.'

On the other hand, I have heard destructive conversations. There were conversations that made jokes of sin. Conversations that made me feel there was no hope for the future; the government is about to fold and the church is going 'to the dogs.' There were remarks that made others look wrong. Then there is the kind of rattling off of foolish chattering that wears you down and makes you feel like pulling your hair. 'Neither give heed to fables, and endless genealogies, which minister questions, rather than godly edifying.' (1 Tim. 1:4)

Builders' Tool Are Provided

Believers are given spiritual gifts to build up the body of Christ. 'It was he who gave some to be apostles, some to be prophets, some to be evangelists, and some to be pastors and teachers, to prepare God's people for works of service, so that the body of Christ may be built up.' (Ephesians 4:11, 12, NIV)

The ability to build comes from God's Spirit gifts. To be an 'upbuilder,' one must allow God's Spirit to work through his life. If you feel you should be more of a builder, let God know your desire. Ask Him to fill you with His upbuilding Spirit; then you can be one who builds others up. You can use your gift, as Paul did, to edify others. Paul wrote, 'But we do all things, dearly beloved, for your edifying.' (1 Corinthians 12:19)

There are many areas where your 'building' gifts can be used. I'll draw attention to several needed ones.

1) Build up one another in Christ. I used to sell eggs to a man who would stand at his front door and talk about Jesus. Jesus was an every day of the week subject for him. We need to daily build up one another in yielding to the Lordship of Jesus.

2) Build up one another in the Scriptures. There are many problems facing us today, and may questions waiting for answers. We need to study the Bible, and build up one another from the insights we gain. We need to be sharing God's principles for living with others.

3) Build up one another on the foundation of the home. Scoffers are being shown on TV poking fun at the home and the God-designed role for mothers. Their poison goes from coast to coast tearing down the very foundations they were brought up on. We desperately need to edify each other in building homes.

4) Build up one another in becoming an active part of the local church. Build respect and supoort for the leaders God chose for the church. Thumbs down on standing in the corner of the fellowship hall talking destructively about the pastor. Build up by personally going to those who have strayed into sin and offended others. Personally and compassionately share yourself for construction of the body of Christ.

5) Build on a personal basis. Be a friend by hearing and sharing the hurts, fears and frustrations of individuals. Be available to the rejected and those outside the 'circle.' Build them up by being a personal friend.

For the redeemed edifiers there is a great reunion ahead. Think of heaven! A gathering of edifiers! A forever convention of positive thinkers! It will be out of this world. It will be so tremendous that this present body won't be able to stand it. We will be given new bodies where we will be enjoying a forever reunion with the Master Builder.

On the other hand, think of hell. It's the reunion of the destroyers, the ones who tear each other down. It's a reunion of those who are accustomed to tearing down one another, tearing others apart, and breaking up relationships for selfish reasons. No wonder the Scripture says, 'There will be weeping and gnashing of teeth.' The destroyers will have forever to rip and gnash and tear at each other. Hell will be hell, because the destroyers will be forever in the presence of the Chief Destroyer, the Devil himself.

I choose to be an edifier. It's more fulfilling here now, and more rewarding in the future. By the power of God's spirit, be an edifier, be a builder! It belongs to the people of God.

Think about this: What would your church be like if you would take edifying seriously? What would it be like if 'edifying' caught on with the group? Wouldn't it be an unusual church? It's an exciting challenge. Make this biblical teaching your goal.

THREE

Kindness Brings Healing

SUPPOSE YOU WOULD HAVE a young son who has a pet collie dog. His dog is one of his best friends. The boy wants to cross the highway and his dog runs ahead into the path of an oncoming car. The dog gets hit and the driver goes on. The boy stands there crushed and wounded in spirit. A strong, husky man comes along in a pickup truck. He stops and gets out, spitting his tobacco juice on the road as he walks toward the boy. Then he asks, "Hey, sonny boy, what happened?" Then he rudely continues, "Oh, it's just a stupid dog. You need to learn the facts of life. What's more, you should have kept him off the road." He spits more tobacco juice and speeds away. The boy is left standing there now with a double wound.

While he stands there crying, another man brings his car to a stop to see what the problem might be. This man pulls the dog off the road, expresses his sorrow, and comforts the boy. Then he asks, "Is your daddy near?" This man gives kind and healing words.

Imagine yourself on the expressway in rush hour traffic. Your tire goes flat and you are without a spare. One commuter pulls over, rolls down the window, and say, "I feel sorry for you." Then he speeds away. Another pulls his car over and hurries to you asking, "Can I help?" The words of one wound your spirit and the others give healing.

There was a man who was traveling from one town to

another. En route he was attacked by thieves. He was robbed, beaten, and left lying by the road seriously wounded. He was likely to die if no help came. He may have been bleeding physically and wounded in spirit. "Will I live? Will I die?" Imagine him as he heard the sounds of footsteps and managed to peep up past his wounds so as to see the silhouette of a priest. Imagine the feeling of hope at the possibility of being rescued. But the footsteps went on by. He was wounded again.

A second time there were footsteps. This time it was a Levite who took a look and passed up the opportunity to offer healing. Finally, the third time a person stopped, saw his need, and out of kindness and compassion applied first aid and healing.

Imagine the wounding of the man's spirit as the two religious persons passed him up and left him to die. On the other hand, think of the feeling of healing in his spirit as the Samaritan applied kindness. Kindness builds up and gives healing to wounded spirits. Rudeness tears down and wounds the spirit of others. It is no wonder that the Bible says, "Be ye kind one to another." (Ephesians 4:32)

Kindness is Commanded

The Bible commands kindness. God wants his people to practise kindness with one another. The New International Version says, "Be kind and compassionate one to another." This kind of kindness is to be practised at the very grass root levels of life. In the home parents are to exercise kindness with their own children. In return children learn kindness toward parents. On the job workers need the kindness of each other. Employer-employee relationships need to be seasoned with kindness and respect. Kindness needs to be extended to those in the church and on every committee. Disagreement is no excuse to violate God's command to be kind, even if it is toward a cantankerous committee member.

Familiarity can become an enemy of kindness. One may think he can be unkind with his wife or brother because they know each other so well. The other person knows you really aren't rude. This builds sloppiness into our manners which is often carried on into public life where your "put on" kindness becomes a phoney veneer. This means you really aren't a kind person, you just have a public front. True kindness is best tested with your best friends and family members. If you do not practise kindness to those closest to you, you really aren't a kind person.

John Drescher gave an illustration to the point in his book *Spirit Fruit.* "A mother developed the habit of being cross and complaining at home. Away from home she was all sweetness and light. One night after she was especially irritable, she heard her child pray, 'Dear God, make Mommy be kind to us like she is to people we visit.'

"At first she felt the prayer was funny. She told it to her husband. He looked at her with a serious expression. The he said, 'You do not treat us with the courtesy you show to the business people and our friends.' It was a turning point for the mother."

Meaning of Kindness

Kindness means usefulness, availability, outgoingness, a generous disposition. The good Samaritan fitted into this description of kindness. So does Jesus Christ, and the man who helps a boy whose dog is killed, or the person who becomes available along the expressway when your tire is flat.

Drescher says, "Kindness is love in little things. It is respect for the feelings and personhood of another. It is thoughtfulness put into action. It is the kind of spirit that builds togetherness and love in situations which could be explosive. Kindness brings blessings and good feeling in the place where bitterness and ill will would flourish."

Kindness is loving and helping another in need. It is conversations that draw attention to the good qualities of others. Kindness refrains from words and remarks which will hurt another or cast doubt on his character. It avoids speaking evil.

Kindness is giving a helping hand and a touch of healing in time of trouble. It could even come in a cup of coffee, tea or milk. A small act of kindness from others has often "made my day." The Spirit fruit of kindness in your life can make the day for others working and living around you. Acts of kindness can be tools in the hands of the Holy Spirit in drawing others to Christ and "making their forever" glorious. Kindness can "make eternity" for others. It can draw them into the family of God.

Exemplified In Christ

Kindness was truly exemplified in Jesus Christ. Paul refers to the kindness of Jesus in his letter to Titus. "At one time we too were foolish, disobedient, deceived and enslaved by all kinds of passions and pleasures. We lived in malice and envy, being hated and hating one another. But when the kindness and love of God our Saviour appeared, he saved us, not because of righteous things we had done, but because of his mercy. He saved us through the washing of rebirth and renewal by the Holy Spirit, whom he poured out on us generously through Jesus Christ our Savior." (Titus 3:3-6) In Ephesians Paul mentions the kindness of Jesus. "And God raised us up with Christ and seated us with him in the heavenly realms in Christ Jesus." in order that in the coming ages he might show the incomparable riches of his grace, expressed in his kindness to us in Christ Jesus." (Ephesians 2:6,7)

Jesus demonstrated kindness in his life as he was on the way to the cross and in his death and resurrection. To the rejected he reached out with kind acceptance. To the blind he kindly gave sight. To the sick he had the touch of healing. To the sinful who came to him he gave wholeness.

In the face of death while he was being stretched out on the cross by the big daring soldiers, he demonstrated kindness. The huge spikes ripped his flesh as the heavy hammers drove them. He was left hanging to die between two thieves as his associates. From that cruel and unjust setting Jesus expressed kindness to the people who administered injustice. For those people he prayed, "Father, forgive them, for they know not what they do."

He expressed kindness to one of the thieves who was dying with him. Jesus spoke kindness to the man hanging next to him who asked to be remembered. He gave an assuring promise; "Today thou shalt be with me in Paradise."

His highest expression of kindness was in his going to the cross. He offered himself to die to take the punishment of my sinfulness. He became the sin offering for me. Through his loving kindness I became a child of God.

To the soldiers, to the companions on the cross, and to us, he was kind. Truly, as the Bible says, "Love is kind." (I Cor. 13:4 NIV) Jesus is our kindness. You are called to pass it on in being kind to others.

It Is Spirit Fruit

"But the fruit of the Spirit is . . . kindness." (Gal. 5:22 NIV) Drescher quoted an old Scottish proverb which says, "Remember if you are not very kind, you are not very spiritual."

Kindness is the opposite of rudeness. Responding with kindness instead of rudeness when one is mistreated is a mark of a truly great person. Foolish, selfish and undisciplined persons lash back at other immature persons who mistreat them.

Drescher wrote, "Kindness is a grace needed everywhere and it can be practised anywhere. Anyone can complain and be rude, only great souls are really kind."

Kindness is a fruit of the Spirit, and comes as a result of our relationship with Jesus Christ. It is not achieved from human resources. Therefore, the spirit of kindness needs to be nourished like a fruit producing tree. Kindness needs to be fed from God's Word and nourished by God's Spirit.

Strong Christians grow in kindness by dealing gently and lovingly with others. They are friendly and kind. They move off the judgment seat and onto the mercy seat. If you deal harshly with others, it indicates you are a weak Christian. It is a sign your kindness fruit lacks nourishment. If you have dealt harshly or rudely, call it sin and confess it to God and the victim. Own and accept your wrong. Then you'll be on your way to maturing in kindness.

Put It On And Add To It

"Therefore, as God's chosen people, holy and dearly loved, clothe yourselves with compassion, kindness, humility, gentleness and patience." (Col. 3:12 NIV) Not only are God's people to clothe themselves and put on kindness, they are further instructed to add kindness. "For this very reason, make every effort to add to your faith . . . brotherly kindness, and to brotherly kindness, love." (2 Peter 1:5a, 7b)

Christians are to be leaders and examples in kindness, yet one often finds the non-Christian to be kinder than the Christian. For example, the busy Christian in a restaurant is often harder to please than the non-Christian. The non-Christian waitress is often kinder in response than the Christian. This is a disgrace to God. Put on kindness, add to it daily and bring honor to your Maker.

How does one practise kindness? I remember my mother had a "kindness voice" when she spoke to the chickens, the cows, and the dogs. She was kind to animals. She practised kindness in the "small" areas of life. She was in turn also kind to people. She spoke very kindly to me.

Practise kindness to the small creatures of life like dogs, cats, and grasshoppers. Don't kick the dog or pull the grasshopper's legs off. Be kind. It will then be easier to respect the rest of God's creation—like your fellowman.

If a young man kicks the dog, he likely won't be kind to his wife. If one is rude to his mother or father, he will likely be rude to his partner. If one isn't kind to old people, he is not a kind person.

Where Does Kindness Grow?

Does it grow and develop by others being kind to you so you can more easily be kind to them? I doubt it. Giving kindness for kindness may not really be true kindness. It may be only responding to kindness.

Kindness really grows where you are treated rudely. Kindness really grows where our life grinds out everyday living. Like responding kindly to your older brother or snobby sister or a sassy clerk. Jesus was treated with cruelty, yet he responded with kindness.

Do I always feel like being kind? No, sometimes I feel like responding with meanness. That's my point of growth. We grow in the Christian grace of kindness when something difficult or rude comes into our lives and we choose to respond in kindness.

Isn't Kindness Weakness?

Weaklings can be rude and nasty to others. It takes strength to be kind. Really, more than I have. It takes God's Spirit strength in me. Kindness is not weakness as some would have us think. While rudeness uses force and can be used by the weak, kindness is actually power.

The story is told of a young lady who worked for an exectuive who was the most cantankerous and critical person in the firm. Working for him was all she could bear. She decided to pay the "old goat" a compliment every day.

The first day she told him, "That's very fine material in your suit." Notice she didn't say fine spirit, but suit. Each day she complimented him on something. She was kind to one with a critical spirit. Finally, the unlovable boss became a lovable man and later her husband.

Suppose you are watching a carpenter drive a nail. He has driven them by the thousand. This time he makes a crooked hit. You say, "Can't you drive a nail?" On the surface, you are kidding. Below the surface, it may be defeating for him. Why can't we notice the total picture of the wall he is building rather than one nail he missed? A kind compliment goes a long way.

True Christians are the ones who began kindness at the cross of Christ. There they begin a change of life and practise kindness. They will grow into kindness and more kindness. They will keep on until they come into the very presence of Kindness. Jesus himself will be Kindness in Kindness City where Kindness music will fill the air. There we will be forever with Kindness.

On the other hand, to not change into being kind may very well end in being in the presence of the rudest person there ever was—Satan. It may end in the presence of a multitude of rude persons who will be rudely gnashing their teeth on one another. That's not for the Christian though. The Christian should reflect on the kindness of God. God is kindness. "Be ye kind one to another."

FOUR

Fulfillment Through Submission

"**I**'M MY OWN BOSS!" I'm going to do as I very well please."
Does that sound like something you've heard before?

Suppose you have just presented ten good reasons
why you should install a certain kind of drinking fountain.
You worked hard to make a clear case on what you are
convinced is right. One catch—the building committee
doesn't go along. It's turned down. "All right," you say,
"I'll not go to the next business meeting."

Have you ever seen two people arrive at an entry and
one urges the other to go first? The other signals, "No,
you go first." Neither really cares to submit to the other.

Are you really your own boss? Is it right to boycott
the business meeting because your ideas weren't all
accepted? What's wrong with submitting to the kind gestures of another?

According to the Bible, "all of you (are) subject one to
another." (1 Peter 5:5) None of us are really our own boss.
If I want to become my best in maturing and serving God, I
must learn to "submit one to another."

The Bible calls us to just that. "Giving thanks always
for all things unto God and the Father in the name of our
Lord Jesus Christ; submitting yourselves one to another
in the fear of God." (Eph. 5:20-21) This call from God is to
be a *thankful* people in the name of Jesus. Being thankful

instead of being an ungrateful and murmuring person then positions you to develop joyfully the second call from God in this passage. It is to "submit to one another in the *fear of the Lord.*"

To submit means to be under obedience, to yield to the authority or will of another, to surrender.

To truly find one's place in life, he must become submissive to authority around him. There are various powers with "whom we have to do." Fulfillment and success come through submission to these authorities.

Highest Authority

The first and highest authority is God. The Psalmist wrote, "Commit thy way unto the Lord." (Psalm 37:5) The New Testament calls for submission to God. "Submit yourselves therefore to God. Resist the Devil, and he will flee from you." (James 4:7) This scripture reminds us that there are two powers. One is God to whom we should submit. The other is Satan whom we are to resist.

There are those who consider themselves not really submitted to God, but then not submitted to Satan either. Not so! We are subject to one or the other. If we are not submitted, we are then subject to Satan and his crowd called the world.

But I'm my own boss, doing my own thing! You are subject to God or Satan. Jesus set the record straight when he said, "He that is not with me is against me; and he that gathereth not with me scattereth abroad." (Matt. 12:30) To entertain the idea of being neutral about submission to God is absurd. Jesus made it clear. If you are not with me, you are against me.

Submission to God and the Lordship of His Son, Jesus, is a serious matter. Those who willingly submit to Him in life will go on to celebrate victory with Him later. God is the winner and the victor. His saints will go to victory with Him. Those who refuse submission now will bow to Him later in judgment. As the Bible says, "Behold, the Lord cometh with ten thousands of his saints, to execute judgment upon all." (Jude 14-15a)

The Bible also says, "That at the name of Jesus every knee should bow . . . and that every tongue should confess that Jesus Christ is Lord, to the glory of God the Father." (Phil. 2:10-11) The point is: Submit to the victor and winner now. Then you'll be part of the winning side on the day of the Lord.

Respect The Elders

The second area of submission is to those who are older. In 1 Peter 5:5 we have this instruction: "Young men, in the same way be submissive to those who are older. Clothe yourselves in humility toward one another, because God opposes the proud but gives grace to the humble." The young upshots who come on the scene and push back the elderly are missing the point. The young educated who "know it all," and nudge out the "elders" with lots of experience are violating one of God's important principles. One who cannot "submit" to an older, more experienced person is holding back godly growth and maturity. Some conflicting situations may not be so much a test of who is right as to whether you can submit to another.

Submit To The Church

The third authority that God calls for submission to is church leadership. "Obey your leaders and submit to their authority. They keep watch over you as men who must give an account. Obey them so that their work will be a joy, not a burden, for that would be of no advantage to you." (Heb. 13:17 NIV) The church is God's people. This family of God must have leaders. God calls for submission so their work will be a joy. It is no advantage to make it a grief or give them a hard time. Even if the leader is in error, more can be accomplished for the sake of truth in the spirit of submission to God-ordained authority than in the spirit of rebellion.

Submit To Government

A fourth authority is government. "Submit yourselves for the Lord's sake to every authority instituted among men: whether to the king, as supreme authority, or to governors, who are sent by him to punish those who do wrong and to commend those who do right." (I Peter 2:13-14 NIV) Submission to these four areas of authority is important in order to become what God wants you to be.

However, to get along in life with others and work effectively, there is one more area of submission we must deal with. It is submitting to one another. "Submit to one another out of reverence for Christ." (Eph. 5:21 NIV) "Yea, all of you be subject one to another. And be clothed with humility." (1 Peter 5:5) This subjection in humility is without pride or arrogance in the spirit of being a servant to the other.

Supreme Example

Jesus is the supreme example of becoming subject to others with humility and in service to others. From childhood, through Gethsemane, and on to Calvary, he was a person of service. En route to the cross he gave himself to humility, subjection, and service. It was there that he gave himself in subjection to God and those around him so that we sinful humans could have redemption. He had the ability to call troops of angels from heaven to destroy his enemies. He is all powerful—yet he submitted himself to the slaughter like a dumb lamb. Because of his love for me he submitted himself to the angry crowd and became as a thief to die.

Imagine you could see far into heaven. There you see Jesus on the throne of glory. He has all the brightness and beauty of God. He needs nothing—for he is in heaven. Imagine seeing a long stairway from God's heaven to this earth. Then Jesus steps from the throne of heaven's security and descends down . . . down . . . down . . into the atmosphere of earth—into the air of cruel humanity. He steps into the midst of a pack of human wolves. Proud and deceitful, liars and murderers await to get hold of him. He, like a dumb lamb, submits himself to die at their hands. He even stoops to wash humanity's dirty feet. Then he permitted these mad, sinful humans to degrade him, nail him to a cross where they could walk by and rail at him. He gave himself in subjection so we can become the children of God. It is this spirit of submission, subjection and humility God is calling us to. "Be subject one to another, and be clothed with humility."

Submission for so many of us is too much. We are so smart and know too much to submit to another. With our education, degrees, and enlightenment submitting to each other is too hard. All too often our one-anothering submission lacks the spirit of a lamb—especially the Lamb of God. Instead, it takes the shape of a rebellious colt that kicks toward the master, rearing and kicking up the dust.

How does this colt kicking work in the church? The church needs to make applications of biblical principles in today's complex world. It needs to give guidelines and raise up a standard to preserve the Church of God.

Test Of Submission

Here is where a test of one-anothering submission comes. The church raises a standard, but a member or two don't feel like following. "I don't agree with it," they say. The response is more like a colt than a lamb. Believers have shown more stubborness to one another on "small" matters of discipline than Jesus did as he descended from his throne down into humanity. Young sisters have rebelled more over a few inches on the hemline than Jesus did in going to the cross to die. Brethren have "kicked up" more over getting *their own way* with haircuts than Jesus did in shedding his blood for your redemption. Kicking up the heels in stubbornness and rebellion to one another, rather than to "submit to one another," mars the blessed Christian fellowship. It isn't worth it!

Does this mean if I disagree I can't say anything and speak my views and feelings? Of course you speak, and ask, and seek. You *appeal* your case and view in the spirit of humility and subjection. In the spirit of a lamb, say, "Help me on this one, I don't really understand." Don't say in the spirit of a mule, "That stupid rule doesn't make sense to me."

Many believers miss a blessing by being too self-sufficient and never needing help. It could be a financial problem or a spiritual shortcoming. If your brothers and sisters offer some financial relief, don't be too proud to submit humbly to receiving. If you are reminded of where you need spiritual growth, humbly submit. If someone reminds you of something that is detrimental to you spiritually, don't kick up your heels, but submit, and grow, and receive a blessing.

Submission Protects You

Why submit to authority? To dad? To the church? To one another? It's your protection from Satan's attacks on your spiritual life. Submitting is coming under protection. Like an umbrella that shields off the rain, so submission shields off or steers away the darts of Satan. If dad says, "I don't want you to go tonight," you had better consider submission. It may be your protection from real harm. If authority says, drive 55, then submission becomes your protector and may make the difference in a pleasant trip or a disappointing occasion. If the church says "no" to some kinds of music, it's in your best protective interest to live in subjection. These authorities are not wanting to be mean or punish, but to protect you.

When you say, "I'm going anyway, Dad," "This stupid rule makes no sense; I won't do it," "It's none of your business what I do" or, "I'm old enough to live my own life," then you move out from underneath your umbrella of protection directly into Satan's firing line. The attacks are not strained or screened by authority. They are not bounced off by the umbrella of authority, but they hit you squarely. Lack of submission accounts for the struggles many believers are having in living joyously and victoriously.

By refusing submission to one another we are saying, "I can do without you. I don't need you." That isn't God's will and plan for our lives. Everyone is subject to someone. It may be that you are subject to yourself. This means you are not in subjection to God and a godly people. If I am not subject to the people of God, then I am subject to the people who serve the devil. If I want to become godly, then I must be in submission to God's people. If you want to be devilish like the devil, then hang around with his crowd and be subject to them. "Know ye not, that to whom ye yield yourselves servants to obey, his servants ye are to whom ye obey: whether of sin unto death, or of obedience unto righteousness." (Romans 6:16)

Think of this—for those who are submitted to God and to each other, "Eye hath not seen, nor ear heard, neither have entered into the heart of man, the things which God hath prepared for them that love him." (I Cor. 2:9)

As for me, I have not fully achieved or arrived yet. However, I do want to keep descending from my arrogant self throne. I want to descend into the fresh, beautiful atmosphere of humility, submission and meekness. There God can more freely do His work through me.

Submit to God and to one another in His Kingdom here on earth. Then on "that day" when you change from this earthly location to the eternal one, you'll ascend from submission into a mansion. From subjection to a banquet in God's presence, where the meek and humble will be exalted, where together they will worship the King of kings, where you'll receive "a crown of righteousness, which the Lord, the righteous judge, shall give me at that day." Submission brings true fulfillment in life.

Submission receives a reward and a crown. How will your case turn out?

FIVE

Divinely Love One Another

FIVE YEAR OLD MARY underwent a serious operation. She had lost considerable blood and needed a transfusion. After checking the rest of Mary's family, the test showed that the blood of her brother matched hers.

"Will you give your sister some of your blood, Jimmy?" asked the doctor.

Jimmy set his teeth and said, "Yes sir, if she needs it."

At once they prepared Jimmy for the transfusion. In taking the blood the doctor noticed Jimmy getting pale, yet there was no apparent reason.

"Are you feeling ill, Jimmy?" asked the doctor.

"No sir!" said Jimmy, "but I'm just wondering when I die."

"Die, gasped the doctor. "Do you think people die when they give blood to someone else?"

"Yes sir!" replied Jimmy.

"And are you going to give your life for Mary?"

"Yes sir!" replied the boy simply.

The Scripture says, "Greater love has no man than this, that a man lay down his life for his friends." (John 15:13)

From *Spirit Fruit*, by John Drescher

The Bible is a love story. It tells the account of the

greatest love ever expressed. That love is God's love for the human race and His personal love for every individual. God loved us while we were yet unloving. Therefore the highest command for His children is to "love one another."

Love—love for one another; it's a command from the Bible. Jesus spoke these words about love: "A new commandment I give unto you, that ye love one another; as I have loved you, that ye also love one another. By this shall all men know that ye are my disciples, if ye have love one to another.

"This is my commandment, that ye love one another, as I have loved you. Greater love hath no man than this, that a man lay down his life for his friends." (John 13:34, 35 and 15:12, 13)

The Bible further states, "Owe no man anything, but to love one another." (Romans 13:8)

"Ye yourselves are taught of God to love one another." (1 Thess. 4:9)

"Love one another with a pure heart fervently." (1 Peter 1:22)

The Epistle of John continues with pointed statements on love. "For this is the message that ye heard from the beginning, that we should love one another.

"And this is his commandment, that we should believe on the name of his Son Jesus Christ, and love one another, as he gave us commandment.

"Beloved, if God so loved us, we ought also to love one another . . . If we love one another, God dwelleth in us, and his love is perfected in us." (1 John 3:11, 23 and 4:11, 12)

To love one another is not an option. It is a command. It is a must in order to be the people of God.

A Special Kind of Love

Love itself has been put in four levels: romantic love, brotherly love, family love and divine love. It is divine love that the Bible calls believers to practice. The people of God can have the inner strength to live in this special kind of divine love. It is called agape love. Divine agape love is the spirit in the heart that will never seek anything but the highest good of his fellowman. It is truly love—not mere emotions. It loves when emotions may be totally absent. Divine love sacrifices, gives and has compassion. Divine love *wills* to love, even if the other person doesn't deserve it. It wills to build up the other, to build good relations, regardless of the cost. It will help when help is not deserved.

Jesus was an example of this kind of love. "But God demonstrates his own love for us in this: while we were still sinners, Christ died for us." (Romans 5:8 NIV)

Bruce Larson related an experience that reminds me of loving the unloving. "At 5:00 on a winter Wednesday I entered New York's Port Authority bus terminal. I was hurrying home for a quick dinner and then on to conduct a mid-week service at a nearby church. The usual crowd was lined up behind the escalators that take suburban passengers to their buses. Briefcase in one hand and newspaper in the other, I got in line and began the commuter shuffle.

Just as I got to the head of the line, a hard-faced middle-aged woman came up from the side, shoved in front of me, planted her elbow in my stomach and stepped onto the escalator.

Now I maintain that there is nothing easy about the Christian life, and every year I see more clearly the complications of radical obedience. What should I say to such a person? I know that I would have said a few years ago—but I am no longer free to put someone like that "in her place." I know what I would like to say. I would like to be a St. Francis kind of Christian who genuinely loves birds and flowers and little children with sticky lollipops and even pushy unloving people in bus terminals.

Being somewhere between my former condition and my ideal one, I removed the woman's elbow from my stomach and said with elaborate sarcasm, "Forgive me, I didn't mean to shove you."

Her reaction was devastating. She turned and, since she was only a step or two ahead, looked me straight in the eye. Her face seemed to fall apart—all her wrinkles changed positions. "I don't understand it," she said with apology and shock. "Why are you so nice to me? I was really rude. I shouldn't have shoved in line like that."

We must have divine love in order to love rude and ill-mannered people, naughty boys, rebellious teenagers and misunderstandings in our relationships with one another.

Let's suppose there is this brother in the church who is faithful to God, his family and the church. He is a regular at every meeting, and can be counted on to help. He'll lead Prayer Meeting, teach Sunday School, work on the building project or help raise funds. He is kind, well-liked, loved and loves others. He is simply a "great guy." His friends flock around him with "God bless you," and "Come for lunch."

Gradually his generosity is being taken for granted. It is assumed he will always be there and do his part. His friends and associates become careless. Someone makes a remark about him that is too much for him to swallow. Being hurt deeply, he withdraws and turns cold. He withholds love, offerings and his help. He turns to worldly friends and is caught buying a six pack at the fast food store. Now it's out—he drinks.

Since that is the kind of man he is, we greet coldly. We lose that cozy, tingling love feeling toward him. Warm emotions have vanished. Now we withdraw. No lunch with him till he straightens up. He blew his cash on worldly friends, don't come crying on my shoulder. He blew it! He knew better! He doesn't deserve love.

Right at the point when he needs love, we withdraw. We act like a dog that got sprayed by a skunk. We leave him. At the time he needs to be encircled with love—his friends step aside.

I know one loses his feeling of love, the emotions do not move you to step over to him and care. It hurts your pride and image. What will others think if you take him and his family to dinner? By human reasoning, he doesn't deserve love.

But this is the very point at which God is calling his people to divine love, the agape, one-anothering love. Giving that kind of love is painful at times. It is unfelt and lacks emotional good feelings. This kind of divine love comes as a result of the will to love. It comes when one decides to do the right acts of love, and wills to act in spite of feelings. Giving this painful love, that is, loving the unlovables, is the point where the erring person will be touched and find it harder to reject and leave such loving people.

Doesn't divine love ever feel emotionally great? Yes, after the painful price! The deeper the pain of love, the greater the victory celebration. The greater the price of giving undeserved love, the greater will be the emotional feeling of rejoicing that follows. Feelings in themselves are not love. Good love feelings are the result of paying the price. Pay the painful price—good emotional feelings will follow.

You may say, I have lost all feelings of love for the other person. There is absolutely no feeling of love left. I give up trying to love the other. This can happen in a marriage relationship, on the job with fellow workers or in the church fellowship. Divine love will love by an act of the will. When feelings have vanished, the person must then love the other by a deliberate act of the will. It will mean loving the other by choosing the right love actions and reactions. This means our actions, reactions and behavior toward the other will be expressions and actions of love. Feelings of love can then be restored. Feelings follow right actions.

Jesus demonstrated an unselfish divine love. He called upon his followers to carry on that same kind of love in the ages to come. He calls believers to love in behavior, actions and proper reactions toward one another. He addressed this pointedly in his Sermon on the Mount. "Ye have heard that it hath been said, Thou shalt love thy neighbor, and hate thine enemy. But I say unto you, Love your enemies, Bless them that curse you, do good to them that hate you, and pray for them which despitefully use you, and persecute you; That ye may be the children of your Father which is in heaven: For he maketh his sun to rise on the evil and on the good, and sendeth rain on the just and on the unjust. For if ye love them which love you, what reward have ye? Do not even the publicans the same? And if ye salute your brethren only, what do ye more than others? Do not even the publicans so?" (Matthew 5:43-47)

How does a person attain this kind of love? Does it simply grow on you at a certain age? Do you receive it by joining church? By a New Year's resolution? A self-improvement course? By turning a "new leaf"? No! Divine love is a Spirit fruit. "But the fruit of the Spirit is *love.*" (Galatians 5:22) And the fruit of the Spirit comes as a natural result, or by-product, of a life that is committed to Jesus Christ and focused pointedly on Him. A one-anothering divine love is produced by being attached directly to the source of love. "I am the vine; you are the branches. If a man remains in me and I in him, he will bear much fruit; apart from me you can do nothing."

Jesus is the source of divine love. When your spirit is "born again" by His Spirit, when His Spirit enters your spirit, or you become attached to His Spirit, then you receive a divine power for divine love. Divine love can only be a result of being attached to the vine of Jesus Christ. By being attached to the vine, the source of divine love, the result then will be the fruit of the Spirit from the very source of love.

Divine love is patient. It hangs in when the going is tough. It sees the other as a potential person for God. It looks past sin and sees the person. It sees hope in others.

Divine love is not jealous or proud. It is happy to see others succeed. It doesn't become upset when others succeed. It helps the other person along in life.

Divine love is not ill-mannered. It is not selfish. It is not irritable. It doesn't keep a record of the wrongs of others. It doesn't keep account of them so they can be used against the other at a later time.

Divine love is not happy with evil, but rejoices in the truth. It doesn't pass on evil about others.

Divine love doesn't give up. It has the hanging-in faith, hope and patience that don't fail.

God's people are called to that high calling of divine love. No wonder the Scriptures call His people to be "grounded in love," "to speak the truth in love," to "walk in love," that love may abound more and more." And that His people should be "knit together in love," and "let brotherly love continue.'

I am aware I do not have the power of my own to love with divine love. But if I walk in fellowship with God, and cooperate with him, asking him to make me into a vessel of divine love, I believe he will do it. As the encouraging words on love in 1 Thessalonians 3:12 and 13 put it, "And the Lord make you to increase and abound in love one toward another, and toward all men, even as we do toward you:

"To the end he may stablish your hearts unblameable in holiness before God, even our Father, at the coming of our Lord Jesus Christ with all his saints."

May the Lord make you to "increase" and "abound" in love.

SIX

Use Hospitality
One to Another

A N INCIDENT HAPPENED when I was about thirteen years old that has stuck with me. One day a salesman came by to see my father. He wanted to sell him an 8-N Ford tractor. The salesman took us in his nice car to the showroom to see his product. I well remember how he stopped by a restaurant to set us up with dinner. Dad wanted to settle for snacks, but the salesman urged him to order a meal. In the end, he sold my father a tractor.

Some time ago a distributing company invited Son Recording, of which I am a part, to attend a display of their products along with dinner at Ramada Inn. What do I remember about the products? Not much! The dinner? Probably a lot more! It was an extraordinary selection of choice, delicate foods. Indeed a rare occasion for me.

These sales people understood a principle. They understood how to entertain strangers and step by step get people to buy their product.

This principle is really taught in the Bible. However, the world's use of it and the Biblical principle are different. The world uses it to manipulate others to do what they want by getting people to dig into their bank accounts and transfer funds over to them.

The Biblical application is different. Christians are to use hospitality to build up one another. It is to be used as a

41

benefit to the receiver. Given to the other without expecting anything in return. Given in the name of Jesus for the encouragement of the other and becoming real friends for the other's good.

Biblical Call to Hospitality

"The end of all things is near. Therefore be clear minded and self-controlled so that you can pray. Above all, love each other deeply, because love covers over a multitude of sins. *Offer hospitality to one another without grumbling.*" (1 Peter 4:7-10 NIV) This is a call for a deep love to each other. Such a love will help us overlook the faults of others, especially in the atmosphere of being hospitable to each other.

The Living Bible says, "Most important of all, continue to show deep love for each other, for love makes up for many of your faults. Cheerfully share your home with those who need a meal or a place to stay for the night."

The Good News Bible says it like this, "Open your homes to each other without complaining."

Elsewhere the Scripture teaches, "Be kindly affectioned one to another with brotherly love . . . distributing to the necessity of saints, given to hospitality." (Romans 12:10a, 13)

Church leaders are to be "given to hospitality," and "a lover of hospitality." (1 Timothy 3:2 and Titus 1:8)

"Let brotherly love continue. Be not forgetful to entertain strangers: for thereby some have entertained angels unawares." (Hebrews 13:1, 2)

Meaning of Hospitality

Strong's definition of hospitality as used in the above verses means to entertain strangers, be fond of guests, lover of hospitality. Friend. Friendly.

Webster's definition: "The practise of entertaining visitors with kindness and courtesy." From these definitions we can get an understanding of what we are to do for one another.

To be a hospitable church means being a loving people who share together in fellowship and food. It means exercising such a fellowship of hospitality. That the drop out will truly miss not being a part. I'm reminded of a friend who was soon to leave to go into foreign service. In fun he remarked to us coworkers that he should be nice to us before he goes so we will miss him when he is gone. That is how true from the heart hospitality works. It is missed when it is no longer experienced. A person doesn't want to leave such a rich love and acceptance.

Too often the opposite is experienced. Believers are at odds with each other to the extent that one or the other wants to leave. We all face crises. But people who use and give hospitality often survive the crisis while others pack up and leave.

Abraham exercised hospitality when three men came to him. For him it meant more than opening the freezer and plugging in the coffee maker. It meant getting water to wash their feet, having Sarah to get ready the three measures of meal, knead it, and make cakes. Abraham ran to his herd, got a tender calf, and had it prepared. He put a lot of work into what turned out to be "entertaining angels." Abraham's actions illustrate the meaning of hospitality. He was given a rewarding word from the strangers; "Sarah thy wife shall have a son." Suppose he would not have used hospitality? See Genesis 18:1-10.

Examples of Hospitality

The Bible gives many accounts of hospitality. Laban to Abraham's servants. Joseph to his brothers when they came to Egypt and he revealed himself to them. Pharaoh to Joseph's father, Jacob, when he arrived in Egypt. Jethro to Moses. Rahab to the spies. The widow of Zarephath to Elijah. The Shunammite to Elisha. Job to the strangers.

Lydia and Paul to Silas. Zacchaeus to Jesus. Jesus at the Passover sharing with the Twelve.

Another striking account happened to two who were on their way to Emmaus. They were talking of the shocking events of the crucifixion of Jesus. A stranger came near and went with them. This stranger inquired about their conversation and sad expressions. One of them asked the stranger if he hadn't known of the things that had come to pass. He asked them, "What things?"

They explained how Jesus was delivered to be condemned to death and that he was crucified. The one they were trusting to deliver and redeem Israel was killed.

As they came to the village the stranger acted as though he was going farther. But the two insisted he stay with them. He stayed and they sat together for dinner (hospitality). The guest then took bread and blessed it, broke it and gave it to his hosts. "And then their eyes were opened, and they knew him; and he vanished out of their sight."

Practical Aspects of Hospitality

Hospitality makes us one. It bonds us to stand together until the day of Christ. It makes us into a family unit. Entertaining guests in our homes enlarges our "family."

But we aren't prepared for guests. There are cobwebs over the fireplace. The floors aren't waxed. The windows aren't clean. I might burn the corn. We aren't fine enough to have guests. I don't know what to say, or their children might mess up the new carpet. To these excuses we need to remember hospitality is not to show our homes, but to share ourselves and express our love with others. Cobwebs and dirty floors will pass. Relationships may last forever. Dirty windows will not always be, but friendships may go on into eternity.

Small deeds of hospitality have deeply touched me. I

recall several from the time I was a partner on an egg delivery route. This one day a young man was home when I came to the door. It was near Christmas and he was feeling the mood of the season. He invited me inside and very generously and kindly shared a ham sandwich with us. Now that's not a big deal, but a small act that stuck with me.

At another time and place, it was late in the day and we were tired and hungry. Smelling food from the customer's kitchens didn't ease the hunger pains. This one customer's family had the most tempting roast on their table. And would you guess—they sliced a big piece and shared it. Both of these incidents have been years ago. There is something about the hospitality at that time that stuck precious memories into my mind. I don't remember if there were any dog hairs on the sofa or cobwebs on the ceiling. I remember the kind deeds.

Those incidents are quite a contrast to what several of my friends experienced . . . My delivery partner came to a customer's house while the man of the house was having a steak. He asked his egg man if he wanted some. Whatever his reply was, the steak-eating man said, "You can't have any." And he didn't give him any. That is a minor incident, and yet it has made a lasting impression, especially when the sight of steak and hunger pains were prepared for at least a taste.

Another friend dropped in on a Christian organization. One of the associates proceeded to give him a tour of the operation. As they began the host poured himself a cup of coffee. The guest also enjoys coffee, but the host never bothered to offer any. So they toured the place, the host sipping his coffee and the guest realizing he didn't have any. Again, not a big deal. But as the saying goes, "It's the little things that count."

One day I received a phone call from a stranger who was interested in visiting one of our churches. Of course I invited him to visit with us. He and his family attended services. After the services he was invited to dinner at the home of our deacon. My family was included in the invitation, and together we discussed faith and our practice of exercising faith. We shared together in conversation, and a good meal. Sometime later I received a letter from this man assuring me that this was the day that changed his life. Christian hospitality and sharing puts grip into the worship service and the sharing of one's faith.

Open your guest book. Look at the last signature. Start backing up the line through the past year or two of guests. Who has been sipping your coffee? Grandma— Uncle Ben—Aunt Sarah—and your good friends. But as you can see, they are your kind of people. Your blood line, your religion, your race and your friends.

There are three classes of people for whom we seldom pour coffee. First, our brothers in faith we've labeled not quite my kind. Too strict, too liberal, too something. The one on your right is too near to being legalistic, so no coffee. The one on the left is too near apostate, so no coffee for him either. The second type of person we seldom extend coffee to is the out-of-our-class. We shy away from the poor ragged ghetto man because his manners are poor, his clothes aren't pressed, and he forgets his deodorant. On the other hand we don't pour coffee for those with a lot more class. We might make a blunder or spill some coffee. The third class we neglect are the unsaved. Our dinner of chicken and fried potatoes with three desserts usually overlooks the unsaved neighbors. While our unsaved friends stay at their house without God, we enjoy our kind of food with our kind of people. Shouldn't you be just the one that makes a special effort to serve your fine God-given food to those others neglect?

I learned some hospitality lessons from my mother. I remember the day when a young Bible salesman came by the house. He was a tired and hungry stranger. Mother shared what she had—milk and homemade pie. For years this man remembered by the way of a Christmas greeting to thank her for the food given him at a time when he was hungry.

Second lesson, her guest book is filled with names of people from many cities who discovered an open door, her good food and friendliness. The poor ragged ones were served as well as those with thousands of dollars worth of trinkets hanging on them.

Why not use our homes as a way of building bridges of friendship? This could be a way of building the kingdom of Christ. This doesn't mean we lose our faith and keep company with the world. It means we would be reaching out to give our fellowman an opportunity to reach for faith too.

Hospitality—it's a process that starts here now, and then extends into eternity. Jesus had encouraging words for hospitality people; "Then shall the King say unto them on his right hand, Come, ye blessed of my Father, inherit the kingdom prepared for you from the foundation of the world: for I was an hungered, and ye gave me meat: I was thirsty, and ye gave me drink: I was a stranger, and ye took me in." (Matthew 25:34, 35)

Hospitality—it's an opportunity to enjoy one another in this life. It prepares you for the great hospitality event which is to come. "Blessed are they which are called unto the marriage supper of the Lamb." (Rev. 19:9) I wonder, if we do not enjoy giving hospitality here, how could we enjoy receiving it there? It's a principle we better learn here, if we expect to enjoy receiving it there. "Use hospitality one to another."

SEVEN

Forgive One Another

WHEN OUR CHILDREN were small we had a yellow and white cat named Fluff. He was a real living animal that made an ideal pet. Our two-year-old could hold him, handle him, and drag him around like no one else in the family seemed able to do. There is nothing like a purring cat for two children to play with. Purring was good music for dad too. Fluff was nice to have around. We all enjoyed him. That is, until he had a bad experience and wasn't able to forgive it.

It happened while we were pouring concrete. Fluff somehow had an accident and got into the wet slopping mixture. Now a nice cat shouldn't have concrete dry and harden on himself.

My wife, out of good intentions and encouragement from me, proceeded to give Fluff a bath. He didn't take to the idea. He threw a fight in order to avoid being stuck into the water. His opposition was so great that he expressed it with a loud scream. Since he was just a cat, we expected he would soon get over it.

Not so! He never got over it. He never forgave us for the bath. We discovered his unforgiving attitude when I tried to get him to purr. We petted him, rubbed his ears, stroked his fur forwards and backwards. He just wouldn't purr. We were concerned that he ruined his "purrer" when he screamed.

He was different otherwise. He wouldn't let my son

49

handle him like before. He was not as pleasant to have around. He wanted to have things his own way. His unforgiveness for the bath against his will made him into an undesirable and suspicious cat.

Life woud have been so much more pleasant for himself and others around him if he could have forgiven. It's too bad he couldn't have overlooked something that was really good for him. Of course he was just a cat. If the silly beast can't forgive, let him rough it out. There is no cat heaven for him to lose. If he won't purr here it really won't matter in eternity.

There was something painful about his unforgiveness. He reminded me of how some people live. His contrary ways remind me too much of some professing Christians I've met. They can't really forgive. They have lost their "purr," their song for Jesus. They are suspicious of others. They can't take rough treatment, and have soon "had it." They become grouchy and unpleasant. Life becomes one big drag.

Fluff never got over his problem. He seemed to nurture his grudge all his life. He failed to become the nice cat he was before. So we just endured life together. As I say, he was just a cat. He could be replaced with another one, and there is no eternity for him to face.

However, you are different. You are created in God's image. You are not disposed of like a cat. You are a person who will exist for eternity. To forgive makes a difference how you live here now, and where you will be spending your eternity.

In his thoughts on life, James wrote, "For what is your life? It is even a vapor, that appeareth for a little time, and then vanisheth away." (James 4.14) The meaning of this is that life at its longest is short. It is like the steam from a tea kettle on Grandma's wood-burning kitchen stove. The steam enters the atmosphere, goes upward and vanishes away. So is life—too short to waste it on nursing grudges and fertilizing hurts. Hell is too long to spend in regretting your failure to forgive.

The Scriptures clearly call believers to forgive one another. It is impossible to be a Christian without receiving God's forgiveness. Therefore, those forgiven by God are expected to forgive others. God forgives our mountains—therefore He expects us to forgive the little hills of others. As the Bible states, "Be ye kind one to another, tenderhearted, forgiving one another, even as God for Christ's sake hath forgive you." (Ephesians 4.32) Again, the Bible says on forgiveness, "Forbearing one another, and forgiving one another, if any man have a quarrel against any: even so Christ forgave you, so also do ye." (Colossians 3.13)

According to *Strong's Concordance*, the meaning of *forgive* as used in the Gospels is to "lay aside, omit, yield up," with the exception of one passage in Luke 6:37 where Jesus said, "Forgive, and ye shall be forgiven." *Forgive* used in the Epistles means to "grant as a favor, pardon." However, the Greek word in Luke 6:37 is much stronger. When Jesus said to forgive, it meant to "release, relieve, dismiss, to free fully, let go, loose, set at liberty."

To forgive in real life today means dropping the charges against the other. Example: You have wronged me. You are a scoundrel. You are a good-for-nothing. To forgive is to drop such charges against another. God dropped the charges against us through the sacrifice of His Son, Jesus Christ. We are scoundrels, but God loves us and sees us as persons that are precious, valuable and beautiful.

To forgive also means canceling demands. Such demands as, "You must confess in tears on your knees, then I'll forgive." "You must give me $50,000 in damages." "You must have new manners." To forgive means to cancel such demands.

On the other hand, forgiveness is not mere toleration, or just putting up with the other, or looking the other way. It is more than politeness, tact, or diplomacy. It is not suppressing or forgetting. It is the painful act of dropping charges even though you are wronged, and cancelling the demands attached to the wrongs committed against you.

Jesus left heaven and came to earth to bring forgiveness. Therefore he had much to say about it. One of his disciples, Peter, asked him if he should forgive his brother seven times. Jesus told him, "I say not unto thee, until seven times: but until seventy times seven." (See Matthew 18:21, 22) After clearly declaring that seven times is not enough, Jesus gave the account of a king who checked on his servants' accounts. One was brought to his attention that owed him millions of dollars. Since the servant didn't have the means to pay his debt, the king ordered him to be sold for a slave, along with his wife, children and property. The proceeds were to pay for the debt. The servant begged for patience from the king with the promise to pay off the debt. The king felt sorry for him, granted him forgiveness and let him go free.

This same servant went out and met up with a fellow servant who owed him about twenty dollars. (Amplified NT) He grabbed the servant by the throat and demanded to be paid. This servant fell down and begged for patience and promised to pay back the debt. The forgiven man refused and had this man thrown into jail until he paid the debt.

This unmerciful action was reported to the king. The forgiven servant was brought before the king who told him, "I canceled all that debt of yours because you begged me to. Shouldn't you have had mercy on your fellow servant just as I had on you?" (See Matthew 18:32-34 NIV) The king became angry and turned the man over to the jailers to be tortured till he repays what he owed.

The seriousness of forgiveness is expressed by Jesus

in the closing statement of this account. "So likewise shall my heavenly Father do also unto you, if ye from your hearts forgive not every one his brother their trespasses."

The charges of sin against us are stacked high. It is impossible for us to pay the debt we owe. If you are a believer, the heavenly Father has forgiven you. Since your high stack of sins are forgiven, he expects you to forgive others their small stacks. It seems to be the little things that "get next to us." Even after being forgiven for such great offenses, it's the stubbles we trip over. Solomon said, "The little foxes, that spoil the vines: for we have tender grapes." (Song of Solomon 2:15) It is often the little debts we allow to spoil our spiritual vines.

Five Points of Forgiveness

1) The need for forgiveness means there has been a broken relationship with the Creator. The Prodigal Son broke relationships with his father. He then needed forgiveness. All humanity is infected with a broken relationship with God. We have "inherited" this broken relationship. It's in "our bones," as the saying goes. Therefore, we need forgiveness with God and with one another.

2) Forgiveness is costly. In Genesis 50:15-21 is the account of Joseph in dialogue with his brothers who had grossly wronged and mistreated him when he was a teenager. Now that their father had died, Joseph's brothers were worried that he would repay them with evil for their terrible wickedness. The brothers sent a message to Joseph seeking his forgiveness.

Joseph had been wronged. His brothers were guilty. They may have *now* remembered how he begged and pleaded with them for mercy when they lowered him into the pit, and when they lifted him out and sold him. The brothers were loaded with guilt for the pain they had inflicted upon Joseph. Now they were in Joseph's hands. He had the power to revenge. What will he do?

His response was with no charges against them and no demand to repay. He restored the relationship at his own expense. He bore the hurt, the prison, the slavery, the emotional pain and the grief. In response he gave them a home and food. In forgiveness you pay and the offender goes free. The offender put out the false reports, ruined your reputation and you suffer. To forgive, you release him and he goes free.

In forgiveness you take the punishment and bear the sentence by standing in for the offender. That is what Jesus did. The cross, the crown of thorns and the five wounds bear witness he stood in sentence for me. Yes, forgiveness is hard. So are other things worth doing. It wasn't exactly recreation and fun for Christ. It was painful and hard. To truly forgive is a power I do not have of my own strength. It must come from the Holy Spirit within me.

3) We must forgive to be forgiven. Jesus clearly taught that, "If ye forgive not men their trespasses, neither will your Father forgive your trespasses." (Matthew 6:14)

4) Forgiveness restores. When the Prodigal Son returned, through his father's forgiveness the relationship was restored.

When there is no forgiveness, when one holds out against the other, relationships are broken. Like two businssmen who feel they have "been taken" by the other. They refuse dealing with each other. It's a broken relationship that means they avoid one another in town meetings, restaurants, and as they pass on the streets. If they attend the same church they'll have to work at avoiding one another as they enter and leave the services. On the other hand, giving forgiveness restores relationships.

5) Live in the spirit of forgiveness. "For thou, Lord, art good and ready to forgive." (Psalms 86:5) Be Godlike— exercise readiness to forgive. God isn't waiting to crack

the whip on you. He is waiting to forgive. You see, Christ has already taken your beating, your punishment. Now the heavenly Father is waiting for the Prodigal to return and receive forgiveness. Like the father of the Prodigal Son, so God is waiting for the offender to come. As God is ready to forgive, so should the offender be ready to forgive.

Years ago I heard the story of two brothers who were builders. As I recall the story, they were roofing a house. They were in a contest to see who could finish his half of the roof first. The one narrowly lost and couldn't swallow the verdict. The response to the incident caused their division. There was not a readiness to forgive.

Let us live in the spotlight of the cross, where we'll constantly be focusing on the forgiveness we have through Christ. Then we won't get caught on the peak of a roof, unable to forgive.

Let us never forget the Father "who hath delivered us from the power of darkness, and hath translated us into the kingdom of his dear son: In whom we have redemption through his blood, even the *forgiveness of sins*." (Colossians 1:13, 14) In Psalms 103:3, David has forgiveness first in the list of blessings from God "who forgiveth all thine iniquities."

God forgives! He expects us to forgive one another.

EIGHT

Comforters in a Hurting World

HAS IT EVER dawned on you that if you want to help someone you must do it here, now? If you want to be useful to others it must be in this present life? Since you have no guarantee of tomorrow, then today is the time to begin being useful to others.

There is a reward for helping others, even for giving a cup of water in the name of Jesus. He said, "For whosoever shall give you a cup of water to drink in my name, because ye belong to Christ, verily I say unto you, he shall not lose his reward." (Mark 9:31) Being able to help others is a unique privilege with a promised reward.

How would you like to be "lifted up" and moved to a place where you could not do anything for anyone? Suppose a tornado-like wind would pick you up, twirl you around, and set you down in a land of "nowhere." A place where you had all you want, but could help no one. You simply could do no good deeds for anyone. Of course that moment is coming when you will not have the opportunity to help anyone. The undertakers handle those cases daily.

God placed us here to help one another. The truly happy and fulfilled people are those who share their lives with others. Those who help others experience a deeper satisfaction in living. Those who have found purposeful

57

living are the one-anothering people.

I notice something else about one-anothering people. They are easier to get along with. They are not quickly angered. They are not as suspicious of others and defensive of themselves. They are enjoying a sense of freedom to live their own lives in spite of criticism from those who live indifferently.

We are living in a world that is racing toward judgment. A world that is constantly talking of war and is involved in fighting nation against nation. A great percentage of the government's budget goes for defense to protect themselves. We have nations prepared to pit bombs against bombs that could blow most of us out of existence. The Bible indicates we are living in a world that "will melt with fervent heat." (2 Peter 3:10)

We are living in a world where people take each other to court and sue if they don't get what they want. They lie one to another to get a few extra dollars. They push each other around to get to the bargain counter. If someone drives their car in front of another, he may hear a horn blowing and see another shake his fist in a rage of anger. People murder others to get their own way and fulfill their inner lusts. Our world is running out of resources while people around the world are hungry and lacking food. The signs point one direction, toward doom and hopelessness. Life is becoming almost as threatening as being on an inner tube in the Atlantic Ocean surrounded by a pack of sharks.

Into such a world of hopelessness God called a very special people. He called a people of hope. These people are the church of the living God. God's people are in a hopeless world called to give hope by comforting one another.

The future of this present world looks bleak. However, for the believer there is comfort. He knows that if it all falls apart, we are assured of coming together again. Notice these assuring words from the Bible. "But I would not have you to be ignorant, brethren, concerning them which are asleep, that ye sorrow not, even as others which have no hope. For if we believe that Jesus died and rose again, even so them also which sleep in Jesus will God bring with him. For this we say unto you by the word of the Lord, that we which are alive and remain unto the coming of the Lord shall not prevent them which are asleep. For the Lord himself shall descend from heaven with a shout, with the voice of the archangel, and the trump of God: And the dead in Christ shall rise first: Then we which are alive and remain shall be caught up together with them in the clouds, to meet the Lord in the air: And so shall we ever be with the Lord." (1 Thess. 4:13-17) Following this passage of hope is the call to God's special people. In a dying world God called his people to "comfort one another with these words." (verse 18)

In the late 1960's, there was a severe flood in Nelson County, Virginia. I was involved in the search for bodies in the debris along one of the river banks. I took pictures of some of the damage done by this flash flood. My daughter, who was around three at that time, was touched and frightened by the stories of tragedy, destruction and death. For some time after that, whenever it would threaten rain or a thunderstorm, she became very scared. She clung tightly to me and asked again and again if it would be a flood. I assured her over and over again that I didn't think so. She was in a frightening world in desperate need of comfort. We live in a frightening world. Its inhabitants are in desperate need of comfort.

David Shank, in a message on comfort said, "Comfort is a universal need, because the condition of distress, disaster, sickness, disappointments, and death . . . are the lot of man everywhere without exception. And it seems that we are so made that as difficult as it is for us to be comforted by friends and those near us, it is even less possible for us to console ourselves.

"And so it is quite normal that one of the tasks that should go on within the fellowship of the Holy Spirit in the life of the congregation of God's people is the ministry of mutual comfort."

Comfort means to give consolation, to console, to encourage, to solace. God's people are called out to give this comfort and be a special comfort-giving people. As the Bible points out, "Wherefore comfort yourselves together, and edify one another. Now we exhort you, brethren, warn them that are unruly, *comfort* the feebleminded, support the weak, be patient toward all men." (1 Thess. 5:11 & 14) God's people are called to be comforters.

Basis for Being a Comforter

1. Live so there is hope. The death of a loved one brings grief. That grief is greatly increased when a friend or relative meets death in an unprepared condition before God. Our foundation of comfort comes from personally living in the hope of a blessed resurrection. The basis for being a comforter comes from knowing that "if our earthly house of this tabernacle were dissolved, we have a building of God, a house not made with hands eternal in the heavens." (2 Cor. 5:1)

Live so that whether by life or death, our life still speaks of hope and comfort. To be a comforter, one needs to live in daily relationship with "our Lord Jesus Christ himself, and God, even our Father, which hath loved us, and given us everlasting consolation and good hope through grace. Comfort your hearts, and stablish you in every good word and work." (See 2 Thess. 2:16, 17)

2. Be assured of hope. We live among doomsday prohpets. Sincere Bible teachers prophesy of the coming calamities and Armageddon. Present day events point toward some climax of history. The age of the computer and electronic gadgets is changing the shape of our lifestyle and future at an alarmingly fast rate. It's mind bog-

gling to keep up.

There is an Armageddon ahead! To give comfort in such a world, we must be assured of hope. We can be comforters if we are assured from the Word that, "nevertheless we, according to his promises, look for new heavens and a new earth, wherein dwelleth righteousness. Wherefore, beloved, seeing that ye look for such things, be diligent that ye be found of him in peace, without spot, and blameless." (2 Peter 3:13, 14)

3. Be a vessel of comfort. Jesus said, "And I will pray the Father, and he shall give you another Comforter, that he may abide with you forever, . . . for he dwelleth with you, and shall be in you." (see John 14:16, 17) We become comforters by being an open vessel to the Holy Spirit. When He fills and overflows us with comfort we are in a position to share that overflowing comfort with others. God's Spirit is the comforter. That comfort often reaches others through His people.

What does it mean to comfort here now? It means to visit the elderly and affirm their personal worth. It means to hear their complaints of arthritis pains and how they can no longer freely move around. It may mean listening to long telephone conversations of one who has hardening of the arteries and heart problems. It means giving assurance that they too are wanted and loved. It may mean giving compassion, understanding, and crying with a couple whose son-in-law is instantly killed. It may mean sharing financially with a brother whose back ailment prevents him from working. It means being understanding and lovingly accepting parents whose son or daughter has turned bad. It could mean to give a listening ear and understanding heart to young people. To give comfort is to care and share with anyone who has a loss or sorrow.

I experienced the meaning of receiving comfort following a house fire on a bitter cold January Sunday. I had preached the morning sermon and dismissed the service.

As I approached the vestibule I was told our house was on fire. I had phoned a neighbor who confirmed the report, and I soon arrived home to witness that the report sure enough was true. We lost the greater part of our belongings as well as basically gutting the house from fire, smoke and water.

It was indeed a comfort to have a good number of the congregation right there helping to board up the remains and do other immediate emergency jobs. We were comforted by neighbors responding with food, clothing, shelter, love and concern. The list of "comforting" could go on and on. In spite of snow, wind, rain and cold weather, six days later our house had a complete new roof. Friends showered us with help which is translated into comfort. The comfort kept coming for days, weeks, and months. I believe this is the kind of comfort the scriptures call God's children to give one another.

Jesus told of a rich man who lived for himself and had no compassion or comfort for others. He wouldn't so much as comfort a begger with crumbs from his table. The dogs gave the poor man more comfort than this rich man. In time the rich man died. Giving comfort was not his life. Now receiving comfort was not his reward. In hell he lifted up his eyes. In life he refused to give comfort. Now he was begging for just a drop of comfort. He was suddenly concerned. He missed being a comforter in life. He missed being comforted in death.

It is different for the Christian who is a comforter. He is accustomed to God being his comforter. He is comforted because there is hope, as the scripture says, "that we through patience and comfort of the scriptures might have hope." He can take great comfort in knowing that sometime God will wipe away all tears from his eyes.

And think about this; your life is either giving comfort or adding misery to others' lives. You are either helping or destroying. God is a great Comforter! Pass it on here now by comforting one another. Be a comforter in a hurting world.

NINE

On Guard In Prayer

HIS PRAYER CLOSET was not a plushly carpeted Holiday Inn. From a less desirable atmosphere he wrote again and again, assuring others of his prayers on their behalf.

To the Philippians he wrote, "And this I pray, that your love may abound yet more." (Phil. 1:9)

To the Colossians he wrote, "For this cause we also . . . do not cease to pray for you." (Col. 1:9)

To the Thessalonians, "We give thanks to God alway for you all, making mention of you in our prayers." "And, wherefore we also pray alway for you." (1 Thess. 1:2, 2 Thess. 1:11)

To the Romans, "Without ceasing I make mention of you always in my prayers." (Romans 1:9)

To Timothy, ". . . without ceasing I have remembrance of thee in my prayers night and day." (2 Tim. 1:3)

The Apostle Paul was a man of much prayer. He prayed fervently night and day. His prayers didn't ascend from a prayer breakfast at a Holiday Inn with a stomach stuffed from an all-you-can-eat buffet. He didn't pay twenty dollars to see some religious celebrities from the electronic church strutting around on the platform displaying their fine suits and glittering apparel and asking to sign a prayer card.

His prayers didn't ascend from a place packed out with the crowd, where the lights are dimmed, the curtain lifts, and the spotlight zooms in on the star attraction. His prayers weren't motivated from the performance that began with a tempo that moved the crowd wildly along with something for everyone.

Such was not the setting in which Paul wrote, "I pray for you night and day." Try to visualize where Paul's prayers came from. In prison, in stocks, in chains. His breakfast—nothing! Pains gnawing in his stomach. Entertainment provided by dirty rats. The spotlight may have been a slight beam of sunlight for a few minutes at high noon. His background music may have been from squeaking bats or other prisoners cursing and swearing. The air was filled with moldy stale odors that would almost take your breath.

Quite a comparison to today's marketing of the Gospel by the performers who get into the "spotlight." At the close of the performance the lobby is jammed to get a closer look and an autograph on a piece of merchandise. All of this is done in the name of Jesus who suffered to give his life for our redemption.

From an undesirable setting Paul wrote and assured the believers of his prayers for them. He is a one-anothering man. He diligently prayed for others, and he requested that others pray for him. He wrote, "Brethren, pray for us," and "Finally, brethren, pray for us, that the word of the Lord may have free course." (1 Thess. 5:25 and 2 Thess. 3:1, 2)

He requested that the Roman believers strive together with him in prayer. "Now I beseech you, brethren, for the Lord Jesus Christ's sake, and for the love of the Spirit, that ye strive together with me in your prayers to God for me." (Romans 15:30)

Paul's instruction to the believers is that I am praying for you—please pray for me too! The meaning of this is, *pray for one another.*

Prayer is a vital part of one's relationship with the heavenly Father and with others. Jesus maintained a life of prayer. He went into the mountain to be alone with the Father in prayer. He "continued all night in prayer." The Jesus kind of prayer builds up one's spiritual relationship with the Father. James wrote, "Pray for one another." (James 5:16) This kind of praying for others also builds up our personal relationships. I can name older people that I know have been praying for me. I consider them to have a vital part in my spiritual development.

The Bible calls believers to prayer. "I will therefore that men pray everywhere, lifting up holy hands, without wrath and doubting." (1 Tim. 2:8) Believers are to be on prayer guard around the clock. "Pray without ceasing." (1 Thess. 5:17) Your life is to be lived in the spirit of prayer.

Jesus spoke a parable that meant, "men ought always to pray, and not to faint." (see Luke 18:1) He instructed that "the harvest truly is great, but the labourers are few: Pray ye therefore the Lord of the harvest, that he would send forth labourers into his harvest." (Luke 10:2)

Pray for one another. God is listening. His ears are open to your petitions. "For the eyes of the Lord are over the righteous, and his ears are open to their prayers." (1 Peter 3:12) The Lord told the prophet Jeremiah to "call unto me, and I will answer thee, and shew thee great and mighty things, which thou knowest not." (Jer. 33:3)

Why pray? Because souls are going to hell! Souls are lost and going to a hopeless eternity where they will be constantly reminded of the opportunities they missed. I am reminded of a pressed and dried flower between the pages of my Strong's Concordance that was apparently put there by my mother while I was a boy at home. When I see it I think of my mother. The flower is a reminder of my childhood days and can stir the feelings of being a child at home. Hell is a constant nagging reminder to its occupants that they missed Christ. Pray on behalf of souls that are headed toward eternity without hope and without Christ.

Why pray? Because the wrath of God is ahead! "And

the heaven departed as a scroll when it is rolled together; and every mountain and island were moved out of their places. And the kings of the earth, and the great men, and the rich men, and the chief captains, and the mighty men, and every bondman, and every free man, hid themselves in the dens and in the rocks of the mountains; and said to the mountains and rocks, Fall on us, and hide us from the face of him that sitteth on the throne, and from the wrath of the Lamb: for the great day of his wrath is come; and who shall be able to stand?" (Rev. 6:14-17) "And they shall go into the holes of the rocks, and into the caves of the earth for the fear of the Lord, and for the glory of his majesty, when he ariseth to shake terribly the earth." (Isaiah 2:19) The wrath of God upon sinful man lies ahead. That's reason enough to pray. Pray for one another to be in Christ, to be sheltered, and to escape God's wrath.

Why pray? Judgment is ahead! The coming of Christ is at hand. The beginning of eternity may be only minutes away! "But the end of all things is at hand: be ye therefore sober and watch unto prayer." (1 Peter 4:7) Pray "because your adversary the devil, as a roaring lion walketh about, seeking whom he may devour." (1 Peter 5:8) With the end of all things being near and the destroyer seeking whom to devour, we should "pray . . . that ye should do that which is honest." (2 Cor. 13:7)

Why pray? That we do not fall prey to unbelievers. Paul coveted the prayers of others, so he doesn't get caught in the unbeliever's snare. "Strive together with me in your prayers to God for me, that I may be delivered from them that do not believe." (Rom. 15:30, 31) Pray for one another that we do not fall into the snare of the unbelievers.

Why pray? We have needs! Some aren't walking with God as they ought. Some aren't ready to meet God. Shouldn't that move us to prayer and have "faith as a grain of mustard seed:" to remove mountains of sins? Jesus reminded his disciples of the importance of prayer after they could not cast out the demon. He said, "Howbeit, this kind goeth not out but by prayer and fasting." Pray and fast on behalf of those who are not ready to meet God.

For what shall we pray? Paul gives us some insights. He made it known for what he prayed. "And I pray God your whole spirit and soul and body be preserved harmless unto the coming of our Lord Jesus Christ." (1 Thess. 5:23)

"Wherefore also we pray always for you, that our God would count you worthy of this calling, and fulfill all the good pleasure of his goodness, and the work of faith with power; that the name of our Lord Jesus Christ may be glorified in you." (2 Thess. 1:11, 12)

Paul wrote to Timothy and gave specifics for what to pray. "I exhort therefore, that, first of all, supplications, prayers, intercessions, and giving of thanks be made for all men; For kings, and all that are in authority; that we may lead a quiet and peaceable life in all godliness and honesty." (1 Timothy 2:1, 2) In Colossians 1:9-11, Paul gave us a model of what to pray for in others. He prayed for them and desired "that ye might be filled with the knowledge of his will, . . . that ye might walk worthy of the Lord . . . being fruitful in every good work, and increasing in knowledge of God, strengthened with all might, according to his glorious power, unto all patience and longsuffering with joyfulness." Pray for teachers and pastors to be "filled with the knowledge of His will."

Pray for the parents of those teenage rebels. Raising a family in a pressure cooker world is a tough task. Guiding teenagers is almost impossible. Pray for parents by name and request "wisdom and spiritual understanding" for them. It is totally scriptural and God's will for them.

Pray for the couple who are experiencing a strain in their marriage relationship and considering separation. Pray that they will be "strengthened with all might.'

Pray for the young people who are being lured by the

pleasures of this world that they "might walk worthy of the Lord."

Pray for the truck driving brother as he meets others, the brethren in business as they deal and trade, the single sisters and widows, that they be "faithful in every good work."

Pray for the young men facing draft registration, for the teenagers who are dating, that they may be "increasing in the knowledge of God."

Oh God, "Strengthen (us) with all might," according to your "glorious power," that we will be honest in a lying world, kind in a rude situation, loving in a violent conflict. Grant that our grandparents will be true models, and our young people faithful. "Strengthen with all might" that our parents will love each other, be faithful and be Christian moms and dads. Grant "patience and longsuffering with joyfulness" to the teacher who will be in charge of my energetic youngsters today.

And finally, Paul includes "giving thanks unto the Father, which hath made us to be partakers of the inheritance . . . who hath delivered us from the power of darkness, and hath translated us into the kingdom of his dear Son." (Col. 1:12)

The scripture calls us to pray for one another. But we are so busy in a rush, rush world. We have *so much to do*.

I understand that years ago the people of Germany were busy. Business was booming, cash registers were clanking, and money was flowing. They owned property and farms. Suddenly the scene changed. They were fleeing from their homes and businesses for survival. In railroad cars, in concentration camps and in prisons they had plenty of time to pray.

We are in a busy world tempted with building a god of wealth and plenty. In such a busy world as ours, seek first to build the kingdom of God by praying for one another. Be on guard for each other.

TEN

Help Carry
the Other's Load

ONE OF THE UNIQUELY different things about a true believers' church is that they help carry the heavy loads of the other. David A. Shank related this experience of one-anothering: "When we were troubled because of having to move, the people of our Christian assembly said to us, 'Just let us know when, and we'll help you.' So within that limited congregation of God's people there was a rapid examination of resources, people, time and trucks. Then over a period of two days, a dozen men each gave a couple of hours of help, and five of the ladies put in a couple of hours of intensive cleaning. One man helped us mow the lawn one last time.

"And so the burden of uprooting was borne with us by a community of people who are committed to us—and we to them—in ways that can make a big difference. You can surely imagine that we are deeply grateful for this kind of community of faith that does not limit itself to brotherly talk, but is close enough to reality to help bear human burdens.

"Someone might even suggest that this is a good illustration of what is implied by the apostolic word to "bear one another's burdens, and so fulfill the law of Christ." (Galatians 6:2 RSV) I am sure that such an action among the people of God is not contrary to Paul's thought and intent. For this is one of the ways of working out the meaning within a congregation of the fact that the baptism of the Spirit not only makes us members of Christ, but also members of each other."

The baptism of the Spirit makes us members of one another. Such members are instructed to "bear one another's burdens, and thus fulfill the law of Christ." (Galatians 6:2 NAS) Burden bearing means "if a man be overtaken in a fault, ye which are spiritual, restore such a one in the spirit of meekness; considering thyself, lest thou also be tempted." (Galatians 6:2) A believers' church is called to carry and endure the burdens and troublesome moral faults of the other. In doing this we fulfill the law of Christ.

What is His law? Perhaps we could say the law of Christ is His principles and reason for coming to Earth. Why did he come and what principles did he bring? Isaiah explains, "Surely he hath borne our griefs, and carried our sorrows . . . he was wounded for our transgressions, . . . bruised for our iniquities . . . with his stripes we are healed." (Isaiah 53:4, 5) His principle is to *bear* our grief and carry our sorrow. Believers are to fulfill that principle.

The Apostle Peter gives further explanation in the New Testament: "For even hereunto were ye called: because Christ also suffered for us, leaving us an example that we should follow his steps." (1 Peter 2:21)

His principle: suffering for the faults of others, bearing our burdens, sins and iniquities. And according to Peter we are called to "follow his steps." The principle of Jesus is our pattern for relationships with others.

Jesus gave a specific word on the law of Christ. He said, "A new commandment I give unto you, That ye love one another as I have loved you, that ye also love one another: by this shall all men know that ye are my disciples, if ye have love one to another." (John 13:34, 35)

The believers' church is called to bear the burdens of

others and thus fulfill this love law. As Jesus explains, "Love your enemies, do good to them that hate you. Bless them that curse you, and pray for them which despitefully use you. And as ye would that men should do to you, do ye also to them likewise." (Luke 6:27-38)

This sounds like a big order. However, if we are yoked, or teamed up with Jesus, we become partners with Him. When we become part of his team, it is not a heavy burden. Take special notice to what he said about the subject, "Come unto me, all ye that labour and are heavy laden, and I will give you rest. Take my yoke upon you, and learn of me; for I am meek and lowly in heart: and ye shall find rest unto your souls. For my yoke is easy, and my burden is light." (Matt. 11:28-31)

As the troubled find rest in Jesus, they discover his yoke is easy and the burden of fulfilling the law of love is not too heavy to bear, especially when this burden is carried by one another.

As we compare Galatians 6:2 with verse 5, one may wonder if there is a contradiction? No, there is not. However, there is an important lesson to be learned. The word *burden* in Galatians 6:5 and *burden* used in Matthew 11:30 by Jesus come from the same Greek word. I share two thoughts on bearing your own burden. (Galatians 6:5)

First, since "bear his own burden" has the same root as Jesus' burden which is light, the lesson can be drawn that each must bear personal responsibility for yoking with Jesus. Becoming one of His disciples is a choice the individual must make. Simply identifying with other believers is not enough. Dad's religion won't do it. Relying on one's heritage, no matter how good, is not enough in itself. Being born into the church, raised in the church, joining the church and being involved will not be enough. Each person is responsible for his own actions. Each must stand judgment alone. Likewise, each must make his personal choice about yoking with Jesus and bearing his burden.

The second thought on Galatians 6:5 comes from the Amplified New Testament. It instructs each to bear their "little load of oppressive faults." Pick up your own ten pounds of faults. Don't expect someone else to do it for you. Repent of your own use of by words. Don't neglect to pay your own debts. Don't be late for your appointments at another's expense. Stop coming to meetings and services late.

It seems to me both of these fit together. If you want to move toward maturity, toward being Spirit-filled and Christ-like, then yoking with Jesus and accepting your own "oppressive faults" is a must. It is imperative that you personally accept your faults, confess them, and change from your own little burdens.

How then do we bear one another's burdens? You pick up your own twenty pound burden first. Then for those who cannot handle their own twenty pounds, help them bear that load. Also there may be one with a one thousand pound load. If a dozen help pick up that one, it means each has less than one hundred pounds.

What are the loads and weights we are to bear for one another? Some very practical ways include helping one who must move. Helping in time of illness or death in the family. It could include inviting the pastor's family for dinner when he is called away for a length of time. It could mean coming to the rescue if one suffers loss by fire, storm or other ways.

I have personally experienced the burden lifting of my load of grief following the death of my first wife. I have personally experienced the burden lifting following a fire that nearly destroyed our house and contents. The church, both local and from other communities, joined by neighbors and friends, formed little armies of help to lift these burdens.

Burden lifting may include helping believers who are

hungry and in need, even though their presence is divided by fields, mountains and oceans. Or bearing the burdens of those oppressed because of their race or nationality. These responses to another's burdens certainly are in order and bear a tremendous testimony of love.

However, there is even a deeper meaning to Galatians 6:2, of bearing one another's burdens. The Amplified New Testament again helps to clarify. It reads, "Bear (endure, carry) one another's burdens and troublesome moral faults." Troublesome moral faults are the burden we are to bear with others. As David Shank illustrates, "It is, rather the burden to be borne by one who has been overtaken with a fault, with a trespass, and is crushed by the weight of the consequences of his action. Bearing one another's burden in that context reaches up to some of the high spots in the midst of the Spirit's work."

Let me illustrate with a member of the fellowship of faith who has trespassed against another, taking large sums of money which he has spent foolishly and cannot repay. Society discovers his crime. He is not only punished, but also required to pay back the stolen money.

Faced with the impossibilities of his situation, it is evident that here is a burden—fully earned and merited, it is true—but which he cannot bear. He regrets not only his punishment, but also his deed. He turns away from his crime, in repentance, and turns from his failure back to Christ and His Spirit of truth.

Paul's appeal is not only to forgive such a member; it is also an appeal to gently restore into full relationships the one who has alienated himself from the new humanity in Christ and from society at large. Yet the burden of assuming personal consequences of his sin is so overwhelmingly impossible that it will continue to keep him in a permanent state of alienation, destroying one who is seen as restored.

And so it becomes clear that the only way to really restore the one at fault is for others to get under the load and carry with with him. The healthy, the whole ones, the spiritual are invited by Paul to "pick up the tab," so to speak, of the faulty trespasser. They are urged by the Apostle to help to carry a load that is too heavy for the one that created it in the first place. They are asked to literally bear his burden and thus fulfill the law of Christ. The work of the Spirit is to restore; and it is only in this way that real restoration can take place.

In reality, the Apostle Paul is asking the congregation to do an unusual thing. The natural thing is to turn one's back on the thief. Paul calls for the extraordinary—the work of Christ—by bearing one another's burdens.

The Church is to be a friend of those who failed. The Body is to bear the burdens of the repentant ones who experience family failure, bankruptcy, too many debts to pay, or involvement in immorality. When such an one repents, can the church truly bear that burden?

Why bear the burdens of others? First, to help him gain spiritual maturity. As Paul wrote to the Colossians, "warning every man, and teaching evry man in all wisdom that we may present every man perfect in Christ Jesus." (Colossians 1:18) In burden bearing we really become peer counselers. It is becoming helpfully involved in the problems of others. Burden bearing is helping people through their problems and on toward spiritual maturity.

Second, burden bearing includes meekly teaching so as to help the other overcome the troublesome moral fault. The Bible gives some helpful instruction on this point, "And the Lord's servant must not quarrel; instead, he must be kind to everyone, able to teach, not resentful. Those who oppose him he must gently instruct, in the hope that God will grant them repentance leading them to a knowledge of the truth, and that they will come to their senses and escape the trap of the devil, who has taken them captive to do his will." (Colossians 2:24-26 NIV)

Third, burden bearing could mean to accompany with

warning. If the person's troublesome moral fault is bringing reproach to the name of Jesus, then in bearing his burden, he must be warned so that person can grow toward maturity in Christ. As Paul wrote, "Brethren, warn them that are unruly." (1 Thessalonians 5:14, also see 2 Thessalonians 3:11, 12) If the other is bringing reproach to the name of Jesus and the church by not paying his debts on time, or performing shoddy and unsatisfactory work, then to be fair to the offender, burden bearing includes giving a warning in the spirit of meekness.

Fourth, burden bearing means giving hope. "Now our Lord Jesus Christ . . . hath given us everlasting consolation and good hope through grace, Comfort your hearts, and stablish you in every word and work." (2 Thess. 2:16, 17)

There is hope in Jesus Christ. He came to give that hope. There is an Old Testament account of a burden bearer named Joseph. His brothers sold him to slavery. Then they planned a big cover up and lied. Twenty years later their sin caught up with them and they were under the mercy of the brother they sold. In Joseph's presence, their burdens were heavy as they feared the revenge he might take. Joseph could have destroyed them. But he didn't. He shouldered their burdens and gave them new hope.

So where do we go from here? Shall we stop the next person we meet and ask if we can lift their burden? No, just quietly and meekly respond when God puts opportunities of burden bearing in your way. Give a listening ear to one that is hurting. Give hope to the one who carries those troublesome moral faults. In this way, bear one another's burdens, and so fulfill the law of Christ.

ELEVEN

Greet One Another

I REMEMBER A particular time that I boarded a plane at Washington National Airport. As my friend and I stepped into the passenger section, we were "greeted" by fellow travelers. Such welcome expressions as "Hello, brother" greeted me as I walked down the aisle locating a seat. It was indeed a warm feeling to be welcomed aboard by fellow travelers going the same direction, to the same city and the same meeting with the same concern. Therefore, there were greetings and rejoicings. We were all enjoying the flight together, as well as taking the same risks. Those greetings from fellow travelers surely helped make my trip a memorable one.

Greeting one another is a practice most people practice to some extent. The practice of greeting is called to our attention in the Bible.

God's people are on a journey moving in a heavenward direction. Their destination is the celestial city. They are en route to a "city which hath foundations, whose builder and maker is God." We are fellow pilgrims somewhat like Abraham and those who died in faith and "confessed that they were strangers and pilgrims on the earth." On our journey from earth to the heavenly city, we pilgrims are to "greet one another." This greeting should have an "urging on" effect on one another. As the songwriter put it, "we're marching to Zion." Yes, we are on the way, greet your fellow travelers, and so help to "make their journey."

It's been my privilege to travel through forty-nine states and a number of Canadian provinces. One of the interesting and exciting things along the way is meeting and greeting others going the same way, or those returning from where we are going.

God's children are moving toward a city. Abraham "looked for a city which hath foundations, whose builder and maker is God." He was a stranger and pilgrim on the earth. Like Abraham, believers are seeking an eternal city. They are en route from earth to heaven. The Bible instructs them to "greet one another" along the way. Peter includes a kiss of love in the greeting. "Greet one another with a kiss of love." (1 Peter 5:14 NIV)

Why discuss the importance of greeting one another, don't Christians already do this? Yes, we greet. Some do it heartily upon meeting and parting with warmth and meaning. Then there are others who need to be found in order to shake their hand.

Greeting one another has meaning. It is more than just the thing to do. In Paul's second letter to the Corinthian Church, he closes the letter with instruction, greetings, and a benediction.

In 2 Corinthians 13:11, he instructs: "Be perfect, be of good comfort, be of one mind, live in peace; and the God of love and peace shall be with you."

Following these instructions for living in verse 14, he wishes them "the grace of the Lord Jesus Christ, and the love of God, and the communion of the Holy Ghost." Now notice what is "sandwiched" between pursuing perfection, being of one mind, etc. and wishing them "the grace of our Lord Jesus Christ." It is verse 11 and 12. It's like a stream of fresh water. It's a source of strength and power. "Greet one another with an holy kiss. All the saints salute you." Greetings equal encouraging, edifying and uplifting each other. Greetings of love are symbols to your brother to keep right on in pursuing perfection and excellence. Greetings can say, hang in there, my fellow heir of the grace of God. To greet in love means to challenge one another lovingly along in the journey to the heavenly city. It motivates and inspires each other to travel on together.

The Apostle Paul sent greetings to other believers and encouraged them to greet one another. Notice the final greetings in his first letter to the Christians in Corinth. "The Churches in the province of Asia send you greetings. Aquila and Priscilla greet you warmly in the Lord, and so does the Church that meets at their house. All the brothers send you greetings. Greet one another with a holy kiss. I, Paul, write this greeting in my own hand. If anyone does not love the Lord—a curse be on him. Come, O Lord! The grace of the Lord Jesus be with you. My love to all of you in Christ Jesus." (1 Corinthians 16:19-24 NIV) To Titus he wrote, "Everyone with me sends you greetings. Greet those who love us in the faith." (Titus 3:15 NIV) Here is a lesson; greet wholeheartedly them that love each other in the faith. Greet with expression those fellow travelers who are marching to Zion. Why do some avoid a hearty handshake—a Christian greeting? Because of the lack of love in the faith, they are not wholeheartedly marching to Zion.

There is a special greeting of love that is expressed by close-knit believers—those who are one in the faith. The Bible calls it "an holy kiss." Believers are admonished to "greet . . . with an holy kiss." (1 Thess. 5:26)

The late Marie Billington saw it as an important practice in expressing Christian love. She wrote, "This symbol of holy love is urgently needed to remind Christians of this part of the full gospel standard. Where Christian people love one another with a pure heart fervently, it is only natural to salute one another with a holy kiss."

In Romans 16:16, the Bible says, "Salute one another with an holy kiss." I personally disagree with the paraphraser who replaces the words *holy kiss* with *hearty hand-shake*. Within the common bond of a community of believers who have committed themselves to the Lord Jesus, and to the upbuilding of each other, it is only reasonable that the expression of love would exceed that of the un-believer, or the one who is not a part of the community of faith.

When is such a special greeting of brotherhood prac-ticed? It certainly would seem appropriate to greet with a holy kiss when this common bond of believers gather for spiritual fellowship.

It would seem proper for those in this spiritual family who haven't seen one another for some time to rejoice in meeting again and to greet in this special scriptural way.

It is a Biblical mandate that those who "have obtained like precious faith with us through the righteousness of Jesus Christ" greet with a holy kiss. It is a badge of the Christian's agape love for brethren to greet brethren and sisters to greet sisters with this special love greeting.

This greeting should be kept special and holy. It should be a dry kiss truly expressing agape love; not a wet kiss which may suggest a taste of Eros love. Editor Ervin Hershberger addressed this in the *Calvary Messenger*, "The holy kiss is a sacred ordinance too sacred to be practiced carelessly. A wet kiss is a slovenly kiss, a careless threat to the sacred ordinance." (C.M., May 1971)

The believer also has a responsibility to those outside the faith community. Every person should be greeted with respect and dignity. After all, Jesus Christ saw value in every person. So much so, that he paid the price of every person's sin.

The Bible points out an important principle of greet-ing others. Third John 14 says, "Greet the friends by name." I think back into my boyhood days to this one particular man's unique handshake. On Sunday morning before Church services began, the youth boys would gather outside. Then just before the services began, we would file inside where we took our seats near the front. During our brief wait outside, many of the older men would file by and greet with a handshake. This one man had the art of making me feel like a person of worth. As he came down the line exchanging his handshake, he spoke the name of the person he was greeting. When he shook my hand, he said, "Simon." That personal greeting did something for me. According to him, I was a person.

The Church should extend a warm handshake and greeting of acceptance to all persons. Treating others with warmth and respect is every believer's duty. To greet visitors and strangers is indeed a unique opportunity to give them a firm message of love and care. Through your greeting let them know they are valuable and important to you. In Jesus' comments on greeting others he said, "And if you greet only your brothers, what are you doing more than others? Do not even pagans do that?" (Matthew 5:47 NIV)

If the believer's warm greeting is reserved for his own circle of close friends, he is missing a golden opportunity of becoming friends to others and of witnessing to God's redeeming love. Expand your circle of friends, greet others, stand in line to meet and greet visitors. Be a visitor welcomer! Don't let them get away without your touch of love.

Jesus gave this warning on greeting, "Beware of the scribes which desire to walk in long robes, and love greetings in the markets, and the highest seats in the synagogues, and the chief rooms at feasts." (Luke 20:46) The teachers of the law were looking to receive greetings and honor. The believer is not to seek to receive, but to give warm friendly greetings to others. The real fulfillment is in greeting others, including the weaker in the faith. Greetings should be extended to the slower pilgrims and strangers who are on their heavenly journey. Greet and encourage those who seem to be sightseeing this present evil world on their journey. Take their hand, encourage them to come along at a faster pace and reach for more maturity.

How do you shake hands and pass on a warm greeting? There are two kinds of handshakes that can be chalked up as bad ones.[1] Ronald L. Willingham has described than as "half gottchi" and "old cold fish."

To shake warmly, don't be a "half gottchi." That is the one when you are feeling for someone's hand, and all of a sudden, before your palms meet, all four of your fingers have been grabbed and hooked in tight. There you stand hurting and hoping for a short ordeal. This one lacks warmth and confidence. Willingham says, "He's usually distant, and standoffish, and doesn't express himself or reveal his feelings." Notice too that this type usually doesn't look in your eyes.

Second, don't be an "old cold fish." Don't just hand someone a mackerel-cold hand and expect him to do something with it. Whoever does that lacks interest in the other. He isn't giving a greeting of warmth and sincerity. It reflects a complete lack of confidence.

How then do you shake hands? Again, Willingham gives some good pointers. "On the other hand, a good, firm, sincere handshake shows confidence, but even more it's a confidence builder. It keeps your level of self-value up and tells everyone, 'I consider myself valuable and important, but I'm just as interested in you.'"

When you shake someone's hand, stand tall. Look him in the eye. Let your hand go all the way into his, until the valley between your index finger and thumb meets the same part of his hand. Clasp his hand in a firm and sincere way. Don't overkill. Quit when you've shaken enough, and be sure you have eye contact with the person you are shaking with.

"Greet one another with an holy kiss." Greet the

friends by name. Warmly shake the hand of your friends and enemies. Pass on a touch of love and celebrate being alive with others. Now is the time to greet and become accustomed to it; because there is a climax greeting time coming. The meeting of the Lord in the air, the gathering of 'all the saints,' the 'voice of the mighty thunderings, saying, Alleluia! for the Lord God omnipotent reigneth.' While we anticipate and wait for the heavenly greeting, practice greeting one another on earth. It's the Biblical thing to do.

[1] Ronald L. Willingham, *How to Speak So People Will Listen*, Word Books, Waco, Texas.

TWELVE

One-Anothering
On The Upper Level

WHILE VACATIONING IN Nova Scotia, our party decided
to ride a ferry boat to visit Prince Edward Island. We
drove our vehicle and camper onto the ferry, then followed directions up the steps to the upper level for the ride
to the Island. The steps were steep, and it took effort to
climb to the top. Upon reaching the upper level the passengers had the opportunity to walk out and observe from
the top deck. There was the opportunity to sit and dine, or
just relax in the comfortable, soft seats of the lounge.
Enjoying the upper level fellowship was indeed better
than spending that precious time below deck among
parked vehicles where there was nothing impressive to
see.

The Christian Church is called the "upper level" of
fellowship. It's the kind of "upper level" that has a taste of
the heavenly. In Paul's letter to the Ephesians, he refers to
"heavenly places." "Blessed be the God and Father of our
Lord Jesus Christ, who has blessed us with all spiritual
blessings in heavenly places in Christ." "But God, who is
rich in mercy . . . hath raised us up together and made us
sit together in heavenly places in Christ Jesus." (Eph. 1:3 &
2:4-6) While these scriptures speak of being seated with
Christ in the heavenly realm, they also suggest to me that
there can and should be a taste of the heavenly places on

the "upper level" of the believers' fellowship while here on earth.

Believers should be a "heavenly" fellowship to each other. Heavenly, because they truly care for each other.

For a body of believers to experience "upper level" fellowship, it will mean climbing the painful steps to the upper deck. These steps are not easy. It means flexing your muscles and putting forth effort to bend those joints with spiritual arthritis. It will not be coasting uphill.

Let us start heading toward the "upper level by examining and climbing these ten additional "one anothering" scriptural steps.

Consider One Another

Step One: "And let us consider one another to provoke unto love and to good works: not forsaking the assembling of ourselves together as the manner of some is; but exhorting one another; and so much the more, as ye see the day approaching." (Hebrews 10:24) The N.I.V. Bible says; "and let us consider how we may spur one another on toward love and good deeds."

When you consider, what do you do? If you are a considerate person, you will stop and take time to hear and consider what the other person has to say.

In a similar way the scripture asks believers to consider each other.

This means to observe fully, to behold, discover, and to perceive. Considering is to try to understand how to spur and encourage the other through their personal struggle and problems. Consider the uncomfortable shoes they must wear, and stimulate them on to love and good deeds. Consider the one that you were about to write off as hopeless. Visualize that person moving through the problem and producing love, helpful deeds, and becoming part of the kingdom of God.

Suppose you have problems considering the other,

and can't really love that person. This calls for some personal repentance on your part. It calls for a private conference with God to explain to Him that you cannot love as you ought. Confess your lack of love, and ask Him to love and accept that person through you. Commit this case to God and will to love no matter how you may feel.

We believers often consider one-another in a similar way children do. They consider each other all right, but the conclusion of the consideration is that if this is the way you are going to play, I won't play. I'm going home, and you just can't play it your way.

The Bible makes it clear we are not to consider each other the way children do. We are to "not give up meeting together." When we don't get along with each other, we all too quickly choose to not meet together any more. If that is the way you are going to be, I'll find another meeting place, or just worship at home. That's Childish!

Don't be like the child that says if you don't play ball my way, we won't play.

The call of the scripture is to meet together, consider the other, watch and discern how to spur others on to love deeds and noble activities. Take the first step to "upper-level" fellowship by considering one another.

Receive One Another

Step Two: "Wherefore receive ye one another, as Christ also received us, to the glory of God." (Romans 15:7) Here is a simple, short, and direct command. Receive as Christ received! "Accept one another, then, as Christ accepted you." (N.I.V.)

The church is called to receive and accept one another as Christ has accepted you. This brings glory to God. To receive means to accept, to take to one's self, to admit to friendship, and hospitality. According to Strong's Concordance it may include leading one aside and sharing food. In a practical application it might mean sitting down to dinner together and enriching fellowship.

Receive is opposite of reject. Can you think of anything worse than being rejected? What feels worse than the feeling of rejection? Rejection contains a taste of hell. Here is why I say that; when a person rejects Jesus Christ, then Christ cannot receive that person into His kingdom. Therefore, on the basis of rejecting Jesus Christ, there is only one other kingdom left for that person, and that is the kingdom of hell. Rejection of Jesus Christ equals hell. Rejection among brothers and sisters equals a taste of hell. There isn't much that feels worse than rejection.

Rejection is lonely.

Rejection hurts deeply.

Rejection wounds one's spirit.

Rejection divides socially.

Rejection discourages.

Rejection ruins children.

Rejection drives people from church.

Rejection divides marriages.

Rejection drives to suicide.

Rejection is Sin!

Jesus is our model for receiving one-another. That can be painful. With Jesus there was no social status to be met, no income barrier, no bank account to match, and no offering pledge required. Jesus didn't require the atmosphere of a sports van, a trans-am shaped piece of metal, gadgets, expensive clothes, or class in order to fit in with Him. "He came *unto* His own, and His own received Him not." That's rejection! "But as many as received Him, to them gave He power to become the Sons of God." That's acceptance.

Christians are a moving people. They travel from place to place indicating that God led them to move. The truth may be they "moved" because they felt rejection where they were in their fellowship.

It is important that we accept others. This does not

mean that we accept and endorse any sins they may be enslaved with. You accept the alcoholic because he is a person. However, you do not accept the sin of drunkenness. Lowering the standard of morality is not accepting other persons. In fact, it cheapens the dignity and value of others.

I had the challenging experience of listening to my cousin personally reveal to me that he was an alcoholic. He kept it hidden through one family reunion after another, and especially from his Aunt Cora. He put on a good front for years.

Today he is living above alcohol. He—the person—was accepted and helped through to victory. The local congregation affirmed his worth by accepting him. Through acceptance he was able to taste of the "upper-level" fellowship that is experienced as we "receive one another."

Forbearing One Another

Step Three: "As a prisoner of the Lord, then I urge you to live a life worthy of the calling you have received. Be completely humble and gentle; be patient, *bearing with one another in love*. Make every effort to keep the unity of the Spirit through the bond of peace," (Eph. 4:1-3 NIV)

Notice the content in which we are admonished to bear with one another. It is presented in the same package with being gentle, humble, and patient. In this bearing with one another we are told to put forth an effort to keep unity and peace.

To forebear means to "put up," bear with, endure. And even suffer for the sake of another person. How much suffering have you done lately for another? When you feel like telling someone to "shut up and ship out", maybe God is telling you to "put up and bear with."

Have Compassion One With Another

Step Four: I was thinking on this subject, I heard a conversation coming from the bathroom where my wife was trying to get our older son to brush his teeth properly. Our two year old, who had learned to put together some vocabulary, was observing his mother and brother. Compassionately he pleaded with his mother "careful with Eldie." He was identifying with his brother's tooth problem. The Bible calls believers to "having compassion one of another." (1 Peter 3:8) This is a call to be sympathetic, kind, and brotherly with each other. It is a call to "love as brethren, be pitiful, be courteous."

The believer is to have compassion instead of repaying with evil. "Not rendering evil for evil, or railing for railing, but contrariwise blessing." (1 Peter 3:9) Give compassion instead of returning evil and insult.

To give compassion is to pain jointly with the other. It is to suffer grief, loss, and distress with the hurting.

Jesus was moved with *compassion*. He saw the multitudes of people being distressed, helpless, and downcast. He compared them to sheep that had no shepherd. He was touched with *compassion* and offered a positive response to his disciples; "the harvest truly is plenteous, but the labourers are few; pray ye therefore the Lord of the harvest, that he will send forth labourers into His harvest." (See Matt. 9:36-38)

King Herod's daughter performed in such a pleasing manner at his birthday party that he promised her anything she requested. She requested the Head of John the Baptist. A sorry king granted her request. John's disciples told Jesus about the sad incident. When Jesus heard this He took off by boat to a place by Himself. However, the crowds followed Him. When Jesus went ashore and saw the huge crowd, He responded—not with the resentment and bitterness—but with *compassion*. In the midst of His sorrow, He felt their sufferings and healed the sick. From a heart of *compassion*, He turned aside the advice of His disciples to send the people back to town for food. Instead, He miraculously fed five thousand men, plus the women and children. (See Matt. 14:6-21) Jesus could have grieved in self-pity over John's untimely and tragic death. Instead He extended heartfelt *compassion* to the crowd.

In another incident Jesus said "I have *compassion* on the multitude, because they continue with me now these three days, and have nothing to eat." (Matt. 15:32)

As He was leaving Jerico, He came to two blind men sitting by the roadside. He had *compassion* on them, and healed them. (Matt. 20:30-34)

Jesus was moved with compassion. Believers are to have compassion one to another. Do you have a young rowdy in the fellowship who continues to drive with a heavy foot? He has been warned by a dozen people almost a total of a hundred times. You knew it was an accident waiting to happen. He failed to keep his racer on the road. A broken leg with six months forced rest. How should you respond? Hurry to his bedside to remind him, "I told you so."? NO! Like Jesus, with compassion. In spite of the hundred-fold warning, the Bible calls believers to the upper level of fellowship by having compassion one of another.

Care For One-Another

Step Five: "There should be no schism in the body; but that the members should have the same care for one another." (See I Cor. 12:21-26)

In a believers' fellowship no one should say about another, "we have no need of you." Each one is needed, and there should be concern about the welfare by caring for one another. There should be no division in the fellowship, but each should care for the other. If one member suffers, all suffer. If one rejoices and is glad, all rejoice and be glad.

The caring in this passage seems to be close to the

same meaning as used in 1 Peter 5:7, "Casting all your care upon him; for he careth for you." Here careth means to be anxious about the other, to care about the other. To a one-anothering people, this means we will be equally anxious about each other. There will be no one left out because of not being as important as another. There should be no splits, no gaps, and no divisions in the body.

In my childhood our family would walk to the neighbors for a visit. Mom and Dad and the older ones were bigger and could walk faster. When I would lag behind I would call for the others to wait for me. Now my own little son expresses his need by saying "carry me." A one-anothering church waits and "carries" for the others so that the entire family of God can move along on their heavenly journey.

On returning from a vacation trip to Alaska, our party was driving through the Dakotas. At this point of the journey we were having serious tire problems. Going down the highway, we could look in any direction and see miles and miles of barren, dry fields. No houses, no service stations, no tire shops—nothing! There was hot weather, mile after mile of dry, barren fields, and the *comfort* of one another.

The church is travelling through a hot, barren, difficult world. She needs to be very sensitive to those who are dropping behind and respond with sincere caring. It may mean waiting on the other, or picking up the other and carrying that one along. If there is one who isn't making it, the stronger ones shall care and pick up the ones who call for help. To care for one-another means becoming a people who pick up each other in order for each one to come along in the family of God in their heaven bound journey. Upper-level fellowship comes through truly caring for one another.

THIRTEEN

Stepping On Towards Heavenly Fellowship

To REACH THE PLATEAU of mountain top experience in Christian fellowship requires work and discipline. As mountain climbing requires painful and risky steps, so does building a strong fellowship of believers. It requires commitment to one-another. Such a commitment includes personal sacrifice and painful steps on behalf of the other. Let us now consider more steps in ascending toward heavenly fellowship.

Minister One to Another

Step Six: "As every man hath received the gift, even so *minister* the same one to another, as good stewards of the manifold grace of God." (1 Peter 4:10) Here the one-anothering word is "minister", or serve. To minister means to serve and give service to one another. To become a New Testament church requires ministering to one-another.

One unique way of serving one-another is to invite others from the congregation to have Sunday dinner with you. This should include families, singles, widows and widowers. (See James 1:27) This ministering to others is an old tradition for some believers, while for others it is a totally lost art. This is a scriptural way of serving others and building up Christian fellowship. If you are not practicing this aspect of social sharing with others, you may do well to make it a part of your ministering one to another.

Ministering, or serving one another, is a gift from God. If the gift of prophecy is important, then so is the gift of serving. Ministering is to run errands, giving assistance, doing little jobs that are helpful in the body of Christ. It may be cutting the grass, starting the furnace, setting up the tables, cleaning up the mess, and removing the cobwebs from the light fixtures. Ministering is being in service one to another. Even though this gift often goes unnoticed, it is a Spirit gift that needs to be exercised.

In reference to the gift of serving, William McRae gives this illustration; "Don't overlook another practical and invaluable aspect of this gift." "It is strange missionaries don't seem to be what they used to be," beamed a speaker, "Take William Carey, for instance. He changed the history of India. We don't have missionaries like that today."

The speaker then spoke of Carey's sister who lay paralyzed in bed for fifty years and could not even articulate her words most of the time. Propped up in bed, she wrote lengthy letters of encouragement to Carey and prayed continually for him.

"If we do not have missionaries like Carey today, it may be because they do not have prayer helpers like Carey's sister."[1]

The tradition of my people has been to respond in service to one-anothering at the time of death in a family. The entire congregation responds to assist, help in any way possible, and give comfort. Being there and caring is ministering and serving.

Ministering includes listening to the problems of others. It is encouraging to the other to express his feelings of depression, and make his emotional need known. To minister may require an hour or two of listening. The depressed will be ministered to, even if you basically just listen.

Jesus ministered to others. He said, "The Son of man came not to be ministered unto, but to minister, and give his life a ransom for many." (Mark 10:45)

Jesus came to earth and became a unique example of what it is to serve. He washed the feet of his disciples, (John 13:1-17) He served at the table, He went to the cross and gave Himself to be a servant.

Those who take this short verse seriously, "minister one to another," are the happy people. They are the ones who are experiencing fulfillment and purpose in living. On the other hand, those who think they should be served are the dissatisfied, cranky, and hard to get along with people.

Live In Harmony

Step Seven: "Be of the same mind one toward another." (Rom. 12:16) "Live in harmony with each other. Don't be proud, but be willing to associate with people of a low position. Don't be conceited." (NIV) To be of the same mind means to "interest oneself in", "earnestly in a certain direction", "set affection on." (Strong's Concordance) God is saying, let's strive to earnestly think in a certain direction. Does this mean that everyone must think alike? If there is any difference at all, are we not a one-anothering church? Do we all have to like spaghetti? Of course not! Paul speaks pointedly to this subject, "Look not every man on his own things, but every man also on the things of others. Let this mind be in you, which was also in Christ Jesus." (Phil. 2:4-5) God is not asking that the Christians think alike on all the ordinary things of life. He is asking the church to get settled on one thing; that is to have the mind of Jesus Christ. Our basic goal, purpose, affection, and direction needs to be Jesus Christ. It means that we choose Jesus Christ to be Lord and manager of our lives.

When we submit to Christ's Lordship, we become

teachable and pliable with each other, thus growing in harmony and relationships. Those who do not invite Jesus to be Lord are inclined to be contemptible and harder to get along with. How sad that religious leaders go through life doing church work and have never discovered the unifying Lordship of Jesus that brings harmony and makes us one.

How cozy for a group of campers to huddle around a campfire on a cold, drizzling, fall night and take in its warmth. On such occasions everyone has one mind; warming by the campfire. We are in a cold, fearful and uncertain world. Let's huddle around Jesus where we will be of the same mind one to another.

Prefer One Another

Step Eight: "Be kindly affectioned one to another with brotherly love; in honour preferring one another." (Rom. 12:10) God calls His people to give precedence and show honour to one another. This is the opposite of striving to receive honour to oneself. It leaves no room for the self-inflated boaster who hangs around bragging on himself and his accomplishments. "Preferring one another" teaches that the other person is worthy of respect, and should be recognized. When this takes place in the body of believers there is a feeling of belonging, being a part of, and a spirit of working together. Preferring and giving honour to one another draws together into a bond of love. This stands in sharp contrast to the selfish person who insists on getting honour for himself. His selfish actions and self honour is a dividing wedge in the body of Christ.

Preferring one another doesn't mean that during Sunday School reorganization you refuse to accept responsibility by "preferring" it to someone else. It doesn't mean that you "prefer" some one else to lead prayer meeting, cut the grass, or clean the basement. This is not a suggestion that we let someone else do the work of the church.

Preferring means deference, courteous consideration, yielding in opinion, submission to the opinion or judgement of another. It isn't courteous to push responsibility that you should be assuming on some one else. It does mean to look out for others, leading the way for them. Preferring one another means to be deeply interested in the other's success. You have a desire for the other to succeed in their Christian life, with their family, and in their business. God's call to the church is to prefer one-another to succeed.

Confess One to Another

Step Nine: "Confess your faults one to another" (James 5:16a) To confess means to acknowledge and agree fully. Agree to your faults, false steps, offenses and sins. Whether they are unintentional errors or willful transgressions, it is in the best interest of the body of Christ to acknowledge and own your own wrongs. Every member should assume responsibility for their own actions.

Refusing to accept one's own wrongs places that person in a sad and hopeless position. It is sad, because it will slowly and surely destroy relationships with others. It becomes hopeless, because it blocks maturing and growing into the likeness and spirit of Jesus Christ.

Marriage partners live with strained and painful relationships because they will not confess their wrongs to each other.

Friends choose to allow relationships to slowly deteriorate by refusing to confess their own wrongs.

Justifying your faults year after year pulls you down, destroys your character, and is damaging to God's reputation. Rather than confessing and owning one's own faults, that person may go as far as starting "another church". Thus we have little churches scattered across our land started by those who cannot bring themselves to admitting being wrong. Can God's blessing rest on such a church?

When we have failed, God calls us to acknowledge and

agree with others on this failure. Own your own faults and failures, nobody else can do anything with them. Failure to own faults puts a stumbling block in the way of others in the church. "Confess your faults one to another."

Members One of Another

Step Ten: "Wherefore putting away lying, speak every man truth with his neighbor; for we are *members one of another.*" (Eph. 4:25)

Being a member means you are part of a body. Maybe a hand, a foot, or fingers; but most assuredly you are a functioning part. First, this scripture verse instructs to *not* lie, but speak the truth. Lying severs relationships. It separates and tears apart. Since the body of Christ belongs to each other, we are not to tear each other apart. Any member of this body is not to be torn away, because we are members one of another.

I recall the painful grinding experience of getting one of my fingers in the knives of a jointer. Rest assured, there is pain attached to losing a piece of finger. The first night was a nightmare. I recall "seeing" pieces of finger lying below the knives with the wood shavings. There was intense pain the first night, coupled with the haunting and lingering question of what the remainder of the finger would look like after it healed.

I remember an experience earlier in life when I fell from a horse. The impact of landing broke my right arm, putting it completely out of joint. I recall going to the doctor, getting the bone reset, and having a cast put on my arm. I took good care of this broken arm. Even a long time after the cast was off I would lay my right arm in my lap while sitting, so to give it special care.

We believers are members of the body of Christ. The local congregation is a family of God that are members one of another. If one of the members becomes severed, dislocated, or wounded in spirit, the rest must work gently toward "resetting" that relationship, or "casting" him toward maturity, or to carefully care for him, and nurturing him back to full strength. This is what it means to be a one-anothering church.

Taking these steps makes a different kind of church. The next step is on the upper level of fellowship: It is called *"fellowship one with another"*. "But if we walk in the light, as He is in the light, we have fellowship one with another, and the blood of Jesus Christ His Son cleanseth us from all sin." (1 John 1:7) The special one-anothering kind of church enjoys this unique "upper-level" type of fellowship. This is a "Koinonia" group. That is a partnership, participation, association, sharing kind of fellowship.

Such a one-anothering kind of fellowship stands in sharp contrast to the fellowship of the world. A truly one-anothering church in this present world is different. If a church is not different from the world it is not the church of God. The two are opposites.

In the world system, lawsuits are the order of the day. Lawyers and attorneys are faring well with a booming business. Someone says the wrong word—the hearer says, "I'll see you in court." Someone who stubs his toe on your front porch may sue you. Wives sue husbands. Husbands sue wives. Children sue parents. It's a sueing world.

A one-anothering people of God stand in sharp contrast to that way of behaviour.

When the load get heavy—the world crushes you down. The church bears one another's burdens.

When you become weak—the world runs over you. The church prays for one another.

When you fail—the world scoffs and writes you off. The church forgives one another.

When you are lonely—the world makes you more miserable. The church practices hospitality one to another.

When you are getting behind—the world rushes away. The church edifies one another.

When you lose your cool—the world returns more of the same. The church loves one another.

When you are on your way to success—the world pushes you down. The church exhorts and encourages one another.

When you strike wrong—the world calls it out. The church considers one another.

When you are different—the world calls you a misfit or retarded. The church receives one another. You are special.

When you are overbearing—the world flushes you out of their circle. The church forbears one another.

When you are learning a hard lesson—the world sneers and says it serves you right. The church has compassion one to another.

When you are poor—the world gives you a bad mark. The church cares for another.

When you are in trouble—the world turns you over to the proper authorities. The church ministers one to another.

When there are problems—the world has a list of suggestions that boggle the mind and require an attorney to interpret. The church is of the same mind one toward another, having the same goal.

When you have a chance—the world grabs it from you. The church prefers one another.

When you are wrong—the world calls it quits and lies about the matter. The church confesses one to another. A biblically one-anothering church is a group of people who, if I fail, will accept me and help me up.

All of this one-anothering equals a special kind of fellowship one with another. My own paraphrase would read, "If we one another in the light as He is in the light, we have fellowship one with another."

A one-anothering people of God who truly care about one another stands in sharp contrast (and I mean sharp) to the behaviour of this present evil world. Are you a biblically one-anothering church?

[1] McRae, William. *"The Dynamics of Spiritual Gifts,"* Zondervan Corp. Grand Rapids, Michigan.

FOURTEEN

Lie Not
One To Another

THERE IS AN EPIDEMIC of lying sweeping over our land. The business man lies to get a dollar. The employee lies on the time card. The manager lies to his employees. The husband lies to the wife, the wife to the husband, parents to children, children to parents and other authorities. The list could go on and on.

In my own experience I recall a minister's wife showing how to arrange a dozen eggs in order to slip in some smaller ones, and still look like a dozen of large eggs. That was arranging a lie.

God looks seriously upon lying. It is a gross sin. In the Old Testament lying was strictly forbidden. "Ye shall not steal, neither deal falsely, neither lie one to another." Very early in the history of God's people, He forbade lying, along with other gross sins such as stealing.

The New Testament commandment is just as strong. "But now ye also put off all these; anger, wrath, malice, blasphemy, filthy communication out of your mouth. *Lie not one to another*, seeing that ye have put off the old man with his deeds." (Col. 3:8-9)

The command of God is simple and easily understood—"lie not one to another." This means no lying among yourselves.

Why address lying? Aren't Christians honest? Perhaps! However, since the Bible clearly teaches its sinfulness, the subject needs to be brought to the attention again and again.

Another reason to address this subject is that it is a problem you and I were born with. (If you don't believe it, ask your mother.) You had learned the clever tactics at a very young age. A third reason to address the subject is that we are living in a world of liars, and need to be reminded that the church is different. In the midst of a lying world, the church is called to honesty and integrity. Therefore, the true church is different in that it is not a group of liars.

You can personally be one of those different people. Being honest in a lying world gives you the privilege to be uniquely different. You can be an extra-ordinary jewel in the midst of a crooked world. You have the opportunity to be a strong character that models honesty and integrity in front of a dishonest world.

The dishonest person becomes like another run-of-the-mill statistic. He drifts off into the lying system of the world and becomes lost in the shuffle like a fish in the ocean.

The honest person is different. Instead of being lost with the rest of the crowd, he becomes a guiding light. You can be that noble minority with outstanding character that "walks honestly toward them that are without," "and provides things honest in the sight of all men," and is "in all things willing to live honestly." (1 Thess. 4:12; Rom. 12:17; Heb. 13:18) You can be a lighthouse guiding others safely to the shores of honesty and integrity.

The Bible points out the seriousness and sinfulness of lying. "Wherefore putting away lying, speak every man truth with his neighbor; for we are members one of another." (Eph. 4:25) "But speaking the truth in love, may grow up into Him in all things, which is the head, even Christ." (Eph. 4:15) To grow in maturity means you must speak the truth.

"Speak ye every man the truth to his neighbor; execute the judgment of truth and peace in your gates; and let none of you imagine evil in your hearts against his neighbour; and love no false oath: for all these are things that I hate, saith the Lord." (Zech. 8:16-17)

"Let the lying lips be put to silence; which speak grievious things proudly and contemptuously against the righteous." (Psalm 31:18)

"These things doth the Lord hate . . . a proud look, a lying tongue." (Proverbs 6:16-19)

"Lying lips are abomination to the Lord: but they that deal truly are His delight." (Proverbs 12:22)

"A righteous man hateth lying: but a wicked man is loathsome, and cometh to shame." (Proverbs 13:5)

"A poor man is better than a liar." (Proverbs 19:22)

Conclusion: The Bible is against lying. It is a deadly sin.

Who Originated Lying?

Where did the lying originate? Who established it? One thing certain, it wasn't God! The Bible declares, "it was impossible for God to lie." (Heb. 6:18) God came and dwelt among us in His son, Jesus, who said, "I am the truth." (John 14:6) So lying had to come from elsewhere.

Jesus told us who originated lying. It was the devil. Jesus explained; "He was a murderer from the beginning, and abode not in the truth, because there was no truth in him. When he speaketh a lie, he speaketh for his own: for he is a liar, and the father of it." (John 8:44)

Satan is introduced lying to the first human beings when they lived in the garden of Eden. He outright lied when he told Eve "Ye shall not surely die." (Gen. 3:4) People have been dying ever since. If you don't believe it, look at the cemeteries and notice the obituary page in the daily newspaper.

Satan brought lying to us. He lies to the unsaved, and makes them believe that they have plenty of time to make peace with God. And if he has his way, that person will never get right with God. I knew a man who sat in a revival service one night while the Holy Spirit was calling him to yield to Jesus. The devil persuaded him to wait until the next night—it would be a little easier. He waited till another night, and another, and another, and his night never came to get right with God by accepting Jesus Christ for his saviour. He was deceived by the devil's lie.

Another lie Satan peddles is that you can be a Christian and live like the world. Take the name of Jesus by profession, but go ahead and indulge in the sins of the world. That's a lie! Being a Christian puts one in sharp contrast to the devil and his world. The Christian life is on a higher level. Don't believe his lies of suggesting otherwise.

Satan lies to Christians. He tries to tell believers that their sins were so big God couldn't have forgiven them. Consequently, many suffer mental anguish and "crack up" under his lies.

Lying is from the devil. He brought it here. He is keeping it going today. He is looking for servants to carry it on for him. If you lie—you are a servant of the devil.

We live in a lying world. While working outside one day, I heard the sounds of tires skidding on the road. A car somehow did a turn-about and skidded down the east bound lane—with the car headed west. Then there was a crash. The driver claimed to be within speed limits. The police calculation and evidences showed otherwise.

I have a good friend who is an upper-level business manager. He told me how he used to lie. Lying was his way of life, espcially when talking on the telephone. He is a believer now and operates honestly.

Husbands lie to their wives. They claim to have been late because of a deadline to meet, when the truth is that they were out with a secretary.

The wife may back the car into a utility pole, and tell the husband it happened when she was in the grocery store. So she lies and collects a hit-and-run case.

Teen-agers smoke pot, hang around with the wrong crowd, and lie to their parents about where they were.

The secretary lies and says, "Sorry, he is not in." while the boss is right there. Clerks lie about the change. Builders lie about the insulation in the walls. Farmers lie about deductible expenses on tax forms. Car salesmen lie about the mileage on the "one owner" this little old lady traded in. Politicians lie about one another. If it is brought to their attention, they explain it away by putting together the right combination of words to make it sound good. This is a lying world.

God's View of Lying

The Scriptures tell us how seriously God takes lying. Take special note of the account in Acts 5:1-11. "Now a man named Ananias, together with his wife Sapphira, also sold a piece of property. With his wife's full knowledge he kept back part of the money for himself, but brought the rest and put it at the apostles' feet. Then Peter said, "Ananias, how is it that Satan has so filled your heart that you have lied to the Holy Spirit and have kept for yourself some of the money you received for the land? Didn't it belong to you before it was sold? And after it was sold, wasn't the money at your disposal? What made you think of doing such a thing? You have not lied to men but to God."

When Ananias heard this, he fell down and died. And great fear seized all who had heard what had happened. Then the young men came forward, wrapped up his body, and carried him out and buried him.

About three hours later his wife came in, not knowing what had happened. Peter asked her, "Tell me, is the price you and Ananias got for the land?" "Yes", she said, "That is the price."

Peter said to her, "How could you agree to test the Spirit of the Lord? Look! The feet of the men who buried your husband are at the door, and they will carry you out also."

At that moment she fell at his feet and died. Then the young men came in and, finding her dead, carried her out and buried her beside her husband. Great fear seized the whole church and all who heard about these events." (NIV) Lying is a serious matter with God.

God doesn't knock everyone over these days for lying. However, He did give us an example that tells us assuredly what He thinks of it. This is a lesson for all ages. All liars shall receive justice at judgment.

Liars Will Believe Lies

Lying has serious consequences for the liar. If he continues to live in lies, he can come to the point of even believing his own lies. "Wherefore God also gave them up to uncleanness through the lusts of their own hearts, . . . Who changed the truth of God into a lie, and worshipped and served the creature more than the Creator." (Romans 1:24-25)

"And for this cause God shall send them strong delusion that they should believe a lie: that they all might be damned who believed not the truth, but had pleasure in unrighteousness." (2 Thess. 2:11-12)

Here is the real tragedy: God will permit the person who practises lying to believe his own lies. It is serious to tell lies, to act out lies, and live a life of dishonesty. God will allow a person to be a liar, and recognize that lying is a choice. Since that is his choice, he then believes his own untruth and will perish in his own unrighteousness.

Gestures Can Be Lies

I remember riding my friend's bicycle after school. I tried riding through a pond that was left in the field from a previous rain. I didn't make it through without tipping over, and I ended up with wet pants. Now the next hurdle was what to tell my mother. That's the same game some politicians have been playing. Rather than outright honesty, it's selecting the right words to cover up at the next press conference. That has been the game ever since you were big enough to use your mind—"What will I tell mother?" That has been the game since Eve ate the forbidden fruit in Eden. This is not the kind of honesty the Bible calls for.

We construe words that aren't outright lies. On the other hand, neither are they the truth. The words may sound truthful and squeeze you through, but in reality it's a lie. You can lie with your eyes, gestures, expressions, or lack of expressions.

The Good News Bible speaks pointedly to this: "Worthless, wicked people go around telling lies. They wink and make gestures to deceive you, all the while planning evil in the perverted minds, stirring up trouble everywhere." (Prov. 6:12-14 TEV)

Judas betrayed Jesus with a kiss. Outwardly it was a gesture of love, inwardly it was a kiss of betrayal. An honest person is not one who practices putting the right words and gestures together to make dishonesty look good outwardly. A person of honesty and integrity is one who lives honestly in words, gestures, and deeds. The life, character, and principles practised by such a person bear out his honesty. The Bible calls Christians to be honest persons, not just honest words and gestures in the right places.

I've heard about people who have wanted to make a believable point call for special attention to what they

were saying. Honest people need not call for such attention. They will not need to say, "Hey, listen to me, I'm
telling you the honest truth." Who ever heard of the
dishonest truth? There is no such thing. Neither does the
honest person need to say, "I'll put my hand on a stack of
Bibles and swear to it." When such expressions are made it
indicates this person does not normally practise honesty
in daily living. It indicates dishonesty is a way of life. The
Bible calls belivers to "walk honestly" and "provide things
honest in the sight of men." (See Romans 12:17, 13:13)

What about telling untrue tales so tall that the listener is expected to know it is not the truth? It's called
lying in fun and "kidding" with the untruth. In social
gatherings the listener doesn't know whether it's playing
with the untruth or if it is honest talk this time. In the
view of the origin of lying, the serious implications with it,
and God's judgment upon it, I consider it as nothing to
play with or do in fun. It does not build character, neither
is it living in the scriptural bounds of "Whatsoever things
are honest . . . think on these things." (Phil. 4:8)

According to scripture lying is sin. In view of the
serious consequences recorded in the book of Acts, I
believe it shouldn't be copied, substituted, or toyed with. It
rots away at the very center of your character like a rotten
apple in a basket of good ones.

The Liar's Future

Liars will be exposed and doomed. They will not "get
by." St. John saw a most desolate future for liars. He
explained their future in the Book of Revelation. "But . . .
all liars, shall have their part in the lake of fire that burn-
eth with fire and brimstone: which is the second death.
And there shall in no wise enter into it any thing that
defileth, . . . or maketh a lie: but they which are written in
the Lamb's Book of Life. Blessed are they that do his
commandments, that they may have right to the Tree of

Life, and may enter in through the gates of the city. For without are dogs, and sorcerers, and whoremongers, and murderers, and idolaters, and whosoever loveth or maketh a lie."(Rev. 21:8,27; 22:14-15) The liar's future is hopeless.

Liars Can Change

If lying is a habit—call it sin. If you habitually handle the truth deceitfully, call that sin too. Repent, confess it to God, and receive His forgiveness. Confess and seek the forgiveness of others to whom you lied. Replace untruthfulness with speaking the "truth in love." Will in your heart to be truthful, and through the changing strength of the Holy Spirit become a truthful person. "Deliver my soul, O Lord, from lying lips, and from a deceitful tongue." (Psalm 120:2)

FIFTEEN

Consume Not One-Another

WE HAD A MINIATURE Collie dog named Julie. She was a lovely little dog that liked to run after the children while they were playing or riding bikes. She wanted to be where her friends were. She even liked being near when the grass was being cut. One day she came too near and got caught in the blades of the rotary mower. I rushed to the scene and saw broken bones and a mauled body. The decision was made that it was best to kill the dog. Painful as it was, that is what we did.

In our relationships with one-another, we don't make decisions like that about another person. However, there might be a comparison with our physical treatment of animals and the way we treat each other when we feel the other person has no further value to us. When we think another person has been wounded beyond remedy we are inclined to write them off or simply let them be destroyed. Personal relationships are too much like the "coon-hounds" that tree a racoon. If that animal comes near the ground, he is mauled to death in a short time.

James Duncan illustrates how we consume one-another. "For several years the church discussed building an educational unit. One family wanted the building in one location while another family felt that another location was more favourable. Each time the proposed building was staked off, the stakes were moved to the other location during the night.

"When this problem was solved through tactful regulations, they disagreed about the kitchen. One family felt the kichen should be included while the other family declared that a kitchen would not be included. The group in favor of the kichen prevailed in the business conference and the building construction began. Soon it was discovered that the kitchen sink was clogged. Further investigation revealed that the drain pipe had been plugged with concrete."[1]

And so the church people continue to consume one-another. The Bible says; "Be not consumed one of another. For, brethren, ye have been called unto liberty; only use not liberty for an occasion of the flesh, but by love, serve one another. For all the law is fulfilled in one word, even in this; thou shalt love thy neighbor as thyself. But if ye bite and devour one another, take heed that ye be not consumed one of another. This I say then, walk in the Spirit, and ye shall not fulfill the lust of the flesh." (Gal. 5:13-16)

Notice verses thirteen and fourteen are "do verses"— "love one another" and "love thy neighbor". Now note that verse sixteen is a "do verse", too. Then following verse sixteen are listed the works of the flesh and the fruit of the spirit. Take special notice that between these two "do verses" is one "do not verse". "Take heed that ye be not consumed one of another." (verse 15)

There is something very significant here. If you "do" the positives in this scripture, you won't be negative. If you love (positive) you can't be hating (negative). If you are building, you won't be destroying. If you are doing the "do verses", you won't have time for the "don't verse" of consuming one another. If a child builds a toy house or barn he won't be pushing over flower pots. "If you keep on biting and devouring each other, you will be destroyed by each other." (NIV)

But if you bite and devour one another in partisan strife, be careful that you (and your whole fellowship) are not consumed by one another." (amplified)

My thoughts go to a group who started a new church in town. It looked like a promising fellowship with a bright future. In several years of time it became a "has been" church. I believe it closed its doors because there was biting and bickering until they consumed one another. This promising group has gone into many directions.

What does it mean to consume? According to Strong's Concordance it means: use up, to destroy.

To use up: that is having "fair weather friends," which means having friends for your own benefit; for what you get out of them. You include them when it is for your own personal advantage. That is how some politicians operate. If it is to their personal benefit, they stand beside another for a photo. To enhance their personal ambition, they are careful who they are seen standing with. They are anxious to pose beside those whom they think will help them. They "use" people for their own ambition. This is "using" a person. That is wrong. The Christians are to be careful not to "use up" each other in this way.

Zacchaeus was a tax collector, somewhat like a present day I.R.S. agent. He wanted to see Jesus. Being a short man, he climbed up into a sycamore tree to get a good view as Jesus went by. Jesus came to the tree, looked up at Zacchaeus, and asked him to come down. He told him, "I must stay at your house today." (Luke 19, NIV) Jesus' primary interest was the person of Zacchaeus for the good of Zacchaeus. The believers' goal should be, "I'll not use you, but be used for your good."

Consume: is to destroy. We destroy one another by continually "hi-lighting" and harping on the weakness of the other. After a while the other may out of discouragement say, "What's the use of trying?" Some believers seem to carry their spiritual high-lighters with them constantly, "hi-lighting" the weakness of the other persons.

Believers are called to affirm the worth and value of persons, and not destroy them.

"The beggar sat across the street from an artist's studio. From his window the portrait-painter sketched the face of the defeated, despairing soul—with one important change. Into the dull eyes he put the flashing glint of an inspired dreamer. He stretched the skin on the man's face to give him the look of an iron will and fierce determination. When the painter was finished, he called the poor man in to see it. The begger did not recognize himself. "Who is it?", he asked as the artist smiled quietly. Then, suspecting that he saw something of himself in the portrait, he hesitantly questioned, "Is it me? Can it be me?" "That's how I see you," replied the artist. Straightening his shoulders the beggar responded, "If that's the man you see—that's the man I'll be."[2] When we visualize something important in others, then we will not be inclined to consume and destroy one another. "Benjamin West described how he became a painter. One day his mother left him with his sister Sally. He found some bottles of coloured ink and decided to paint Sally's portrait. In the process he messed up the kitchen. When his mother returned, she said nothing about the kitchen. Picking up the paper he was working on, she exclaimed, "What! It's Sally!", and she rewarded his effort with a kiss. West said "My mother's kiss that day made me a painter."[3]

Consume means to waste. If a one hundred thousand dollar house burns, it goes up in smoke as it is consumed by the flames. When we consume one-another we are destroying and bringing it to naught. Several Old Testament scriptures will help us to grasp the meaning of consume. In Numbers 1:11, the word is used. "And when the people complained it displeased the Lord . . . and the fire of the Lord burnt among them, and consumed them that were in the uttermost parts of the camp."

Again in Numbers 16:21, "Separate yourselves from among this congregation, that I may consume them in a moment." The critics of God's chosen leader, Moses, were "consumed". The earth opened up and swallowed them and they went to the place of the dead. The earth consumed them. To consume and bring each other down is forbidden in scripture.

Causes for Consuming One-Another

Selfishness. I want to have my own way. I am not actually involved in living out the "doing" scriptures of loving one-another and my neighbor as myself. When this love dimension is missing, I am selfish.

When you become selfishly interested in yourself, you must protect what you have, live so others will speak well of you, preserve your reputation, and fight to stay on top.

What happens to such selfish persons? In protection of themselves, they consume one-another.

"I didn't get my share of the apples" (or whatever) "I'll get you back next time." Consume!

"What you said insulted me, and you are not getting by with that one." Consume!

"I'm not getting my share of the credit for what's being done round here, so I'll pass on some not-so-nice information about those who are getting the credit." Consume!

"I didn't get the position I wanted, so I'll start another church." Churches that start from strife often consume one-another.

"You didn't pay me enough, so I'll get you back." Consume!

Selfishness is a root cause for consuming one another.

There are other ways to consume others. I will briefly mention six of them.

1. Busybodies. There are several scriptures that address this subject. They will be helpful in discerning how to not be busybodies. "But let none of you suffer as a murderer, or as a thief, or as an evildoer, or as a busybody in other men's matters." (I Peter 4:15) Notice the association here. Busybody doesn't sound so bad until you take a close look at where God's word puts the warning. It is with a murderer and thief. This implies it is serious to be a busybody. "For we hear that there are some which walk among you disorderly, working not at all, but are busybodies." (2 Thess. 3:11)

It is quite evident that those "busybodies" were not working for the cause of Christ, but were the ones destroying the church and consuming one another. Paul writes of those "wandering about from house to house; and not only idle, but tattlers also and busybodies, speaking things which they ought not." (I Tim. 5:13) Busybodies gossiping from house to house destroy and consume others. "Without wood a fire goes out: without gossip a quarrel dies down." (Proverbs 26:20 NIV)

2. Perversity. Perverse is persistance in doing wrong. It is the person who says, "I know it's wrong, and I shouldn't do this. I don't care. I'm going to do it anyway." This is destructive to the body of Christ. "For I know this, that after my departing shall grievious wolves enter in among you, not sparing the flock. Also of your own selves shall men arise, speaking perverse things, to draw away disciples after them." (Acts 20:29-30) Speakers of perversity consume others as they make mock confessions of "I know it is wrong," and then go on and spew out their poison. Paul instructed Timothy how to respond to "perverse disputing of men of corrupt minds, and destitute of the truth." He wrote, "From such withdraw thyself." (See 1 Tim. 6:3-5)

The church is called to be "blameless and harmless, the sons of God, without rebuke, in the midst of a crooked and perverse nation, among whom ye shine as lights of the world." (Phil. 2:15) Believers are to build up, and not consume.

3. Hatred consumes. Lack of love brings hatred. Hatred is destructive. "For we ourselves also were sometimes foolish, disobedient, deceived, serving divers lusts and pleasures, living in malice and envy, hateful, and hating one another." (Titus 3:3) Again, notice the sins associated with "hatred". It is listed with other destructive evils. "Hatred stirreth up strife, but love covereth all sins." (Proverbs 10:12)

4. Pride consumes. "Only by pride cometh contention: but with the well advised is wisdom."

"Pride goeth before destruction, and a haughty spirit before a fall." (Proverbs 10:13; 16:18) Our selfish pride consumes others.

5. Scorning consumes and destroys. This is making fun of, or mocking the other person. "Cast out the scorner, and contention shall go out, yea, strife and reproach shall cease." (Proverbs 22:10) If a person needs to be corrected, do it in a polite and mannerly way. Do not scorn and destroy in the process.

6. Wrathfulness destroys. "A wrathful man stirreth up strife: but he that is slow to anger appeaseth strife." (Proverbs 15:18) The New Testament speaks pointedly to this subject. "Who is a wise man and endued with knowledge among you? Let him shew out of a good conversation his works with meekness of wisdom. But if ye have bitter envying and strife in your hearts, glory not, and lie not against the truth. This wisdom descendeth not from above, but is earthly, sensual, devilish. For where envying and strife is, there is confusion and every evil work." (James 3:13-16) Follow this thought: strife equals confusion, confusion equals evil works, evil works equal destruction, destruction is consuming one another. Jesus said, "and if a house be divided against itself, that house

cannot stand." (Mark 3:25) If there is a divided house in the body of Christ, we cannot stand. If there are those stirring up strife and envyings, we cannot stand. We cannot be a destroyer and build the church of God.

Don't Be a Destroyer—Be a Builder

Don't consume one another; be a restorer. I have personally helped in a number of building projects. It was a pleasure on occasions to take friends by and show them the project I helped build. I have also helped to tear down several houses. I do not recall ever taking special effort in taking friends to the spot and showing them how we tore down a house. There is nothing artistic or honourable about being a destroyer. However, there is a certain amount of dignity that goes with building something worthwhile.

There is something honourable about building the church of God. And God is calling us to be builders in His kingdom. Those who are active builders are the growing Christians. They grow as they help others grow. Those who are not builders do not grow much either. Those who consume one another are also being consumed.

Jesus called believers to be restorers and to help rebuild. "Moreover, if thy brother shall trespass against thee, go and tell him his fault between thee and him alone: if he shall hear thee, thou hast gained thy brother." (Matt. 18:15) If your brother has transgressed, you are to personally to become involved in restoring. Jesus gives further instruction, "But if he will not hear thee, then take with thee one or two more, that in the mouth of two or three witnesses every word may be established." (verse 16) If the offender has not heard you alone, then take along another to plead and work for restoration. If you are not being heard, then "tell it unto the church." When a member of the family of God has erred, we must not consume, but work *together* at restoring that person to fellowship.

Some wanted a kitchen in the new church building project, and some didn't. One day the drain was clogged. It was discovered that there was concrete in the drain. That is consuming and destroying one-another. Be careful not to consume, destroy, or use up one another.

For me, being careful is not enough. I want to go beyond that. I don't have the inner strength within me to be careful enough. I need a greater strength. How do I get it?

First, it means coming to God and opening my life to Him. It may include getting away in a secret closet, closing the door, and doing some business with God. "God, I can't be careful enough, will you show me where, when, and how I am consuming another. Show me how I may be destroying their character, reputation, personage, and personality. I'm open for your Spirit to correct me." As I come in commitment to God, I expect the Holy Spirit to convict and show me areas to correct.

Second, I must seriously seek out the Word of God. As I read and study, God may speak directly to my very present need. Teach me thy word, O Lord. Pray for the Word to teach you.

Third, as I do this, it allows God to develop conviction that consuming and destroying is wrong and sinful. Just about the time that "funny" story is being told, the Holy Spirit may convict to hold off.

Fourth, I must confess to God when I detect my actions and attitudes are destructive. "God, I have sinned. I need your cleaning and straightening up process.

Finally, replace the attitude of strife with *actions* of love. "God, take the strife out of my heart, and give me strength to give actions of kindness and love.

Really, this issue of consuming one-another means each of us must do our personal business with God in a personal manner. We must allow and seek for God to build conviction in your heart and life, so it will make a difference where we live. Therefore, you will "not consume one-another."

[1] Duncan, James E. Jr., *Relax and Let God*, Broadman Press.
[2] Schuller, Robert, *You Can Be the Person You Want To Be*, Pillar Books.
[3] Drescher, John, M., *Seven Things Children Need*, Herald Press.

SIXTEEN

Speak Not Evil
One Of Another

THERE WAS A MAN who went to Europe. "When he came back, all he could talk about was the fact that his hotel window in London wouldn't open. He never saw the greatness of London, or Paris, or Rome. The vast Atlantic didn't impress him. A stuck window!"[1]

A person can become so engrossed in the faults and dislikes of others that he loses the glow and upbeat of life. You can become so obsessed with another's 'stuck window' that you miss the beauty of the Christian life. The result of getting stuck on another's 'stuck window' is speaking evil of that person. Speaking evil of another is destructive to the body of Christ. It tears apart and divides. It's little wonder than that the Bible commands believers *not* to speak evil of another. "Speak *not* evil one of another, brethren. He that speaketh evil of his brother, and judgeth his brother, speaketh evil of the law, and judgeth the law: but if thou judge the law, thou art not a doer of the law, but a judge." (James 4:11)

The New International Bible gives another slant to this verse. It reads, "Brothers, do not slander one another." The Good News Bible says, "Do not criticize one another, my brothers." The message is clear and threefold: Do not speak evil, slander or criticize one another. When you do you are not keeping the law, but sitting in judgment of the law.

The meaning of the word *evil* as used in James is to slander, circulate false reports to damage another's reputation, to speak against, to talk against. So the person who is constantly 'yacking' about another is generally not enhancing the other's reputation. Instead it is being damaged, and to this the Bible declares, "do *not*" do it.

"He that uttereth a slander is a fool." (Proverbs 10:18) "Anyone who speaks gossip is a fool." (TEV) We believers do not want to make statements that belittle others. We are in the body of Christ. When we gossip evil reports, we tear off pieces of the body. We don't yank off spiritual arms and legs at once, but small bits of fingers and hand, slowly and surely, until the arm is destroyed. We may even get a piece of his 'hide' and distribute it. Gossip is passing on information intending to hurt others.

It is not gossip to share a concern for another when you are willing to risk your own reputation in order to help that person. Getting information in order to be a more effective rebuilder is needed at times, but it should *never* be used to 'speak evil' of the other. Seeking information and counsel for helping the other is different from passing on information that may be damaging. Jesus put his life on the line for the sake of others. Information about others should be received in the same spirit of reconciliation.

The Bible gives us incidents of slander. Joseph was slandered and spoken evil of by Potipher's wife. Naboth was slandered by Jezebeel and Jeremiah by his own people. Jesus understood what it meant to be spoken of in an evil way. He was accused of being a wine bibber, and with blasphemy.

Slander or accusing is characteristic of the devil. It comes from him and is rooted deeply in his character. Revelation indicates that he "accused them before God night and day." (Rev. 12:10) He accuses you when he has the opportunity. Therefore, we have learned accusing from the devil. It's no wonder then that the Word of God says, "Speak not evil one of another."

Notice the scripture passages that address the subject and forbid it. "Thou shalt not raise a false report: put not thine hand with the wicked to be an unrighteous witness." (Exodus 23:1) Don't even put yourself in the company of evil speakers.

Ministers' wives are to guard against slandering. "Even so must their wives be grave, not slanderous." (Titus 2:3)

"Put them in mind," Titus is told, "to speak evil of no man." (3:1,2)

"Let all . . . evil speaking, be put away from you. And be ye kind one to another, tenderhearted, forgiving one another, even as God for Christ's sake hath forgiven you."(Eph. 4:31,32) Evil speaking is a definite no-no. Instead, there is to be kindness and forgiveness.

"Wherefore, laying aside all malice, . . . and all evil speakings, as newborn babes, desire the sincere milk of the word, that ye may grow thereby: . . . Having your conversation honest among the Gentiles: that whereas they speak evil of you, as of evildoers, they may be ashamed that falsely accuse your good conversation in Christ." (1 Peter 3:16)

There are several important principles in these passages. First, scripture teaches us to stop speaking evil, that destroys. Second, we stop speaking evil so we may grow and become upbuilding. Those who speak evil of others are not only hurting others, they hurt themselves too. It prevents their own growth toward maturity. It reveals a lack of strong character, will power, determination and insights into tough problems.

Why do 'evil speakers' lack these important qualities? Because they focus on the weakness and problems of others in a destructive manner. They focus and highlight the problems and faults of others, and leave themselves out of the examining picture. Therefore, they do not see their own needs. They become like the photographers who do not see their own peculiar posture as they are focusing on the prize image. Consequently, they do not grow; they remain weaklings. The meaning of Peter's message is to stop this kind of activity and grow up yourself.

Evil speaking may simply be a leveling process. The evil speaker realizes the other is more mature in making sound judgments and wise decisions. It's like he is several rungs higher on the spiritual ladder. Then the evil speaker pulls him down in order to put them both on the same level. While they may appear to place both on one level, it is most destructive and growth stunting to the one who speaks evil.

Consequences of Evil Speaking

It separates friends. "A froward man soweth strife." (Proverbs 16:28) When clique groups whisper to themselves so as to exclude others it causes separation of friends.

It wounds. "The words of a talebearer are as wounds." (Proverbs 18:8)

It causes strife. "Where no wood is, the fire goeth out: so where there is no talebearer, the strife ceaseth." (Proverbs 26:20)

It promotes murder. "For I have heard the slander of many: fear was on every side: while they took counsel together against me, they devised to take away my life." (Psalm 31:13) Slander is so serious it can lead to loss of life.

God's Negatives Are Positive

When one refers to a forbidden act in the Bible, the accusation may be raised that it is a negative book. Others may claim that being a Christian is negative, because you can't have fun and indulge in certain pleasures. I take issue with that thinking. Sure, the Bible does forbid certain things and acts of behaviour. That doesn't mean it is negative. God's *don'ts* are really positive.

There are two reasons why I believe that. First, violation of 'negatives' produces harm to yourself. To violate a *do not* harms the violator. It can bring physical, psychological, emotional or spiritual damage. Your body is designed to receive God's best. When you violate you hurt yourself. God's "no-no's" are positive, because God knew it would hurt you. Therefore it is forbidden.

Look at the young man who indulges in fornication with whosoever he can find at the time. Will he suffer? Of course! No way he can violate God's law and come out winning. Physically he is opening himself to the latest in VD. Emotionally he is damaging himself if he ever does want to settle down. There is no way that he can skim the cream off the top and waste it, then return to find it still there. Some marriages are almost impossible because the cream was skimmed before marriage. Others experience trouble because of the emotional involvement from earlier illicit experiences.

Lying will ruin a life. You can overload your conscience and become hardened to God by continual lying. It can earn you a failure on earth and hell forever.

Holding a grudge can actually make you sick. Mack Douglas wrote, "Five minutes of hate equals eight hours of work."[2]

God's "no-no's" are really positive. When we "lay aside every weight and sin which doth so easily beset us," we are free to move up the ladder of maturity.

Evil speaking as well has its consequences. Dr. S.I. McMillen, MD, wrote, "Most of us do not retaliate against others by pounding our heads on the floor or grinding our teeth together. Neither do we shoot one another or give doses of rat poison. That isn't Scriptural—or legal! The most common way people get even with others is by talking about them . . . Running people down does not keep us free from a host of diseases of body and mind. The verbal expression of animosity toward others calls forth certain hormones from the pituitary, adrenal, thyroid, and other glands, an excess of which can cause disease in any part of the body. Many diseases can develop when we fatten our grudges by rehearsing them in the presence of others."

Secondly, the Bible is positive because it calls you to positive action. There are over a dozen positive "one anothering" actions in the New Testament; such as love one another, edify one another, etc.

While the Bible commands to not speak evil, it also calls for a positive speech. "Let no corrupt communication proceed out of your mouth, but that which is good to the use of edifying, that it may minister grace unto the hearers." (Ephesians 4:29) I was visiting with my neighbor, and in the course of the conversation, I gave a simple compliment about something I appreciate about her. To this she replied, "You made my day." God calls us to a positive speech that helps "make the day" for others.

Notice the positive aspects of speech in the Book of Psalms and Proverbs. "Whoso offereth praise, glorifieth me: and to him that ordereth his conversation aright will I shew the salvation of God."(Psalm 50:23) "The mouth of a righteous man is a well of life: In the lips of him that hath understanding wisdom is found. (Proverbs 10:11 & 13)

"A soft answer turneth away wrath: but grievous words stir up anger. The tongue of the wise useth knowledge aright: . . . a man hath joy by the answer of his mouth: and a word spoken in due season, how good is it!" (Proverbs 15:1-4, 23)

"A word fitly spoken is like apples of gold in pictures of silver." (Proverbs 25:11)

In these scriptures are some principles. Speak something worthwhile, or be silent. If you can't speak to a person, don't speak about him to someone else.

Tim LeHaye related a story how he saw this principle in action. "As I submitted to an airport examination before boarding a plane, the security officer began to criticize the individuals who flew on the airline as "slovenly, inconsiderate, disarranged, and ungrateful people." I took it just about as long as I could, but finally, looking at him with a big smile (I find one can say almost anything if he smiles) I observed, "You must be an unhappy man!" He looked at me rather startled and replied, "Why do you say that?" "Because you're so critical. I've never met a happy person who is a critical person." After inspecting my baggage, he said, "Thank you, sir, I needed that." To my amazement he turned to the next customer and said, "Hello, how are you? So glad to have you on our airline."[4]

"Let your speech be alway with grace, seasoned with salt, that ye may know ye ought to answer every man." (Col. 4:6) Our speech is to be seasoned with flavor and grace. God's grace to us is hope. Our speech should be seasoned with hope. When in conversation with others, they should feel a sense of hope being uttered by our words. Our words should contain hopeful acceptance of other persons so they can say to themselves, "I think that I too can make it." All too often our conversation lacks the flavor of grace and the other person feels condemned.

Perhaps by now you are saying to youself, "I don't have this kind of speech. It must be for a chosen few who have the knack of it." I'm sure there is a difference in all of our spiritual gifts, and for some it flows more naturally than for others. However, the challenge is how much of a priority do you make "speech . . . with grace, seasoned with salt?" If it does not become a priority of which you practice regularly, then there will be no progress in developing graceful speech. Make it a priority by seeking out scriptural help and reading helpful material on the subject.

In listening to one's own speech, the reminder comes through—"I need to change." The good news is we can change. The Spirit of God brought a change in the speech patterns of a disciple of Jesus named Peter. He changed from a liar to a mighty communicator of the Good News. That changing power is available for us today, "because greater is he that is in you, than he that is in the world." (1 John 4:4) This is not a call for you to "try to do better." It's a call to submit yourself to God's Spirit, ask and allow him to make you a person with excellent speech. He is able to give you speech that does not speak evil of others.

[1] T. Cecil Meyers, *Living on Tiptoe*, Word Books.
[2] Mack Douglas, *Success Can Be Yours*, Zondervan.
[3] S.I. McMillen, *None of These Diseases*, Fleming H. Revell.
[4] Tim LaHaye, *How to Win Over Depression*, Zondervan.

SEVENTEEN

Grudge Not
One Against Another

ONE SATURDAY NIGHT I was preparing for a sermon and didn't get to bed until after midnight. Then around two o'clock that night I was awakened by our little dog. I didn't get up at that time to see what her problem was, then about four A.M. I was awakened again and got up to check on her. I discovered she had given birth to three puppies and was now needing some extra attention. In checking on the dog, I discovered she couldn't stand or walk. As the rest of the family discovered the sad state of their pet, I realized that we must do something for her. So, off to the vet they went in the early hours of Sunday morning. As expected, it was a rather expensive visit to the vet with a dog that was mean anyway. Thinking over the entire experience, of being awakened from a much needed rest, and costing me plenty to keep a sassy dog alive, I still find it in my best interest to not hold a grudge against the dog, the dog owners, (who were the children), or even the wife who preferred not to get rid of the dog.

Holding a grudge against another doesn't belong with God's people. Very early in the history of God's called-out people, He commanded them to not hold a grudge toward toward each other. "Thou shalt not avenge, nor hold a grudge against the children of thy people, but thou shalt love thy neighbor as thyself." (Lev. 19:18) The message

133

here is, no grudge—but love. It is clear that grudges and love are opposites.

James wrote, "Be ye also patent: *stablish* your hearts: for the coming of the Lord draweth nigh. Grudge not one against another, brethren, lest ye be condemned: behold, the judge standeth before the door. (James 5:8-9)

What Is A Grudge?

Grudge: what is it? Secret ill will in resentment of a real or fancied wrong. Fancied wrongs are ideas that aren't really true. I have imagined things that I thought were done against me, only to find out that they were not true, after all. So why grudge?

Grudge means to give with invisible reluctance, or to give with regret. To put a twenty in the offering plate and inwardly regret to see it go is giving grudgingly. That may be why God's Word says; "Every man according as he prospereth in his heart, so let him give; not grudgingly." (2 Cor. 9:7)

Grudge is ill will, spite and murmuring. Maurice Wagner described it like this: "A grudge is a hostility in a deep freeze."[1] Hostility is when I feel you are bad, and I don't need you around. It's deeply frozen and well preserved. This means it can be pulled out any time, and be given a quick micro-wave thaw, then be used against the other person. In street language, such a grudge is "a chip on your shoulder." In the language of Bible translators to not grudge means: "Don't grumble . . . one against another." (RSV) "Don't make complaints one against another." (Phillips) "My brothers, don't blame your troubles on one another." (NEB) "Do not complain." (NAS) "Don't grumble." (NIV)

Why Not Grudge?

Why not grudge? When you do you are taking revenge into your own hands. This indicates that you are on the throne of judgment. You do not trust God's judgment to take care of everything. So John did say something nasty about you! Grudge means you want to measure out judgment and justice. You must aid God to work it out in John's best interest. You are afraid God will be too busy and not give him what he deserved.

Therefore, when I carry out a grudge, I want to carry out vengeance by getting even. I'm not ready to forgive. Instead I want to make the other pay up. "Vengeance is Mine, I will repay, saith the Lord." Grudging is wrong because vengeance belongs to God, and not to me.

It may be true that one gets a lot of satisfaction out of grudging. I feel good because I made the other person pay, and suffer as much as I did. But it is a false satisfaction and very short lived. It gives no inner assurance of peace and forgiveness from God. It doesn't give a deep, inner satisfaction nor happiness. Have you ever seen anyone truly happy after they forced the other person to pay up?

Again referring to Wagner's comments, "A grudge is a hostility in a deep freeze. It takes only an instant under the heat of a similar situation to thaw out the old anger and to begin acting out in an accelerated way all the feelings that have been held back for years." Grudges are old feeling reserved for future use to get even with the other. When the moment strikes, your anger thaws then for immediate use. Grudges and hostilities are people centered. You generally do not take out grudges against trees and other things. It is mandatory by the very nature of the Christian life that a believer cleans up his relationship with others. As the Bible explains, "Let all bitterness, and wrath, and anger, and clamour, and evil speaking be put away from you with all *malice*: and be ye kind one to another, tenderhearted, forgiving one another, even as God for Christ's sake hath forgiven you." (Eph. 4:31-32) Grudging is contrary to the very nature of the Christian Life.

You May Be The One At Fault

Don't grudge—you may be the one at fault yourself and may fall under judgment. The grudge one carries may simply be revealing his own weakness. It reveals the kind of person and the character that you really are. Therefore, the grudger simply can't stand the begrudged because he sees too much of his unliked self. The grudges one carries often reflect the very acts and deeds of our own lives.

Grudges will bind you to the one you hold your grudge against. When one has a grudge against another, he thinks he is going to be free from that person and go on doing his "own thing". That isn't true. The one who carries a grudge is not free. He is bound and tied to the person he begrudges. He becomes a slave who is constantly driven by a slave master.

Here is how it works: the one you begrudge is on your mind. That person runs your life and decisions. He becomes your driving force. I'm not going there—because he is going there. I'm not buying any because he did. I won't eat any—because he offered it. I don't need help-from him. I won't own a Chevy—he has one. I won't go to that doctor—he did. He eats catsup on french fries—so I won't. Since he drinks Coke—it's hard on your teeth. He sells Amway—so I'll buy Shaklee.

To carry a grudge burdens you to a constant alert of passing on vengenace to the other. You are not free to live and do as ye ought. The person you begrudge is controlling you. You are wasting your thoughts, energies, actions, and reactions in revenge. The chip on your shoulder is weighing you down.

Dr. S.I. McMillen, M.D. addressed this in his book, "None of These Diseases." "The moment I start hating a man, I become his slave. I can't enjoy my work anymore because he even controls my thoughts. My resentments produce too many stress hormones in my body and I become fatigued after only a few hours of work. The work I formerly enjoyed is now a drudgery. Even vacations cease to give me pleasure. It may be a luxurious car that I drive along a lake fringed with autumnal beauty of maple, oak, and birch. As far as my experience of pleasure is concerned, I might as well be driving a wagon in mud and rain.

"The man I hate hounds me where ever I go. I can't escape his tyrannical grasp on my mind. When the waiter serves me Porterhouse steak with french fries, asparagus, crisp salad, and strawberry shortcake smothered with ice cream, it might as well be stale bread and water. My teeth chew the food and swallow it, but the man I hate will not permit me to enjoy it."[2]

Solomon's observation was similar: "Better a meal of vegetables where there is love, than a fatted calf where there is hatred." (Prov. 15:17, N.I.V.)

Grudging is Destructive

Why not grudge? It may cause you to destroy others. Like Herodias who had a quarrel against John the Baptist, "and would have killed him; but she could not." (Mark 6:19 see chapter 6:14-29) As a result of her grudge, John was executed, and his head was brought to her as requested. Holding a grudge can lead to murder.

Why not grudge? It destroys yourself. Grudges knock me out spiritually. I can't preach as I ought. As the Bible says, "Lest ye be condemned." Carrying a grudge is a condemning feeling. McMiller wrote, "Many diseases can develop when we fatten our grudges by rehearsing them in the presence of others." Grudges put you into an emotional distress. This in turn is destructive to yourself. Emotional stress can cause or aggravate a list of physical ailments, including ulcers, high blood pressure, headaches, diabetes, allergies, backache and heart diseases.

It Can Make You Sick

Holding a grudge can make us sick. Many people who visit the doctors are not really ill, and a pack of prescribed M&M's may make them feel better. My aged foster grandfather was too feeble to continue attending church services. This one Sunday it was my turn to stay with him. During this time my neighboring friend came by the house. Being young boys we decided to play "doctor" with Grandpa. When my parents came home from church he told them that the doctor was there, and he felt better. That, of course, was only momentary cure for his problems. And so it is with curing grudges with pills. It is very short lived.

It Could Kill You

Holding a grudge could kill you. T. Cecil Meyers relates: "Several years ago I knew a man who was very sick, and although the doctor had examined him carefully, he couldn't find anything wrong organically. But one morning he died. When I asked the doctor what killed him, he replied, "Hate." Then he went on to explain that years before this man had had a misunderstanding with another man whom he never forgave. He talked about his hurt constantly, and died of hate."[3]

It's Expensive

There is a high price to pay for holding a grudge or getting even. Dr. McMillen included an entire chapter on, "The High Cost of Getting Even." The opening illustration states the case well. "I received much inspiration for this chapter from Dale Carnegie's account of a trip to Yellowstone Park, and a visit to the place where the Grizzly bears are fed. He did not have to wait long before a Grizzly bear came into a clearing where garbage had been dumped to entice him. The guide told the group that the Grizzly bear can whip any animal in the West with the possible exceptions of the Buffalo and the Kadiah bear. That night, as Dale Carnegie sat with the other tourists in the bleachers, he noticed there was only one animal the Grizzly would allow to eat with him— a skunk. Of course the Grizzly could have won in any fight with a skunk. He resented the skunk and yearned to get even with him for his brazen impudence. But he didn't. Why? Because he knew there would be the high cost of getting even."[4]

Get Rid of It!

Holding a grudge has a high price attached. It is in your best interest to "get rid of it."

This requires doing some business with God. Go to your private closet to make "settlement" with God from the very depth of your heart. The following is the kind of business you should be doing with God:

1. Agree with God—grudging is sin.

2. Acknowledge God's sovereignty, His holiness, justice, and right to taking care of vengeance. Turn the "getting even" over to the God of justice. Hand it over to Him like a ball leaving the pitcher's hand. Then commit your inner desire to do vengeance to the begrudged over to God.

3. Forgive from your heart. Release that person from all "getting even" demands you have chalked up in your mind. As you drop the demands, accept by faith that God can manage His own good will in your life and the life of the other.

4. Ask God for His forgiveness and cleansing. Since He freely forgives a repentant person, accept His forgiveness and be free.

5. Let God know, "I want a complete turn about. Fill me with your spirit of love so there is no room for the spirit of getting even."

6. If your grudge has marred or wounded relationships with others, go restore that relationship through

confession and seeking forgiveness.

It is in my best interest to "grudge not one against another." God has given a power bigger than my grudges—it's called Spirit power. It is available to empower the believer to live in victory over grudges.

[1] Maurice E. Wagner, *"Put it All Together"*, Zondervan.
[2] Dr. S.I. McMillen, M.D., *"None of These Diseases."*, Fleming H. Revell.
[3] T. Cecil Meyers, *"Living On Tiptoe"*, Word.
[4] Dr. S.I. McMillen, M.D., *"None of These Diseases"*, Fleming H. Revell.

Meet the Author

FROM COUNTRY TO CITY ... tasting sorrow and finding victory a simple life committed to Christ ... and a desire to spread the Gospel ... these are all characteristics of Simon Schrock of Fairfax, Virginia.

Born in 1936 in Oakland, Maryland, to Amish parents, Simon became a Christian and a member of the Amish Mennonite Church. During his childhood years, he knew the serenity of life in rural Appalachia, attending a one-room school and a country church.

After his marriage to Eva Lena Yoder, Simon moved to the Washington D.C., area and felt the contrast of the smoky, noisy city. He soon began passing out Christian literature as he moved about the city. The death of his young wife led him through some deep soul-searching, but ultimately deepened his commitment to Christ. Pauline (Polly) Yoder and Simon were married about a year later. They have three children.

In 1968, Simon was introduced to evangelization through Christian bookrack ministry. He began dreaming of good literature for travelers through the Washington National Airport, and placed his first inspirational books in the airport during that year. Since 1968, Simon has been instrumental in the sale of over 220,000 books at two Washington airports. [Choice Books is now providing

141

Christian paperbacks in the public market from Maine to Florida.]

This manuscript grows out of Simon's concern to provide wholesome, inspirational reading material to the public. He lives on the cutting edge of his own denomination and participates fully in evangelistic outreach through preaching, writing, and speaking engagements. It is from this perspective that Simon writes. He is a warmhearted Christian whose life exemplifies what it means to live in obedience to Christ.

He has written over one hundred articles published in Christian periodicals, and has authored two other books, *Get on With Living*, and *The Price of Missing Life*.

—*Herald Press*

One-Anothering Cassettes

cassette player not included

Nine cassettes with 17 messages in a 10-pocket vinyl album. Recorded live at Faith Christian Fellowship, Catlett, VA. These recordings contain the original messages from which the book **One-Anothering** was compiled.

- Hear the messages in the author's own voice.
- Listen while driving to work, etc.
- Loan to shut-ins.
- Great gift idea.
- Satisfaction guaranteed.

Produced and sold by:
Son Recordings, 4614 Holly Ave., Fairfax, VA 22030   (703) 830-2801

ORDER FORM

Please send me _____ One-Anothering Albums.

$28.95 each _____

VA residents add 4% sales tax _____

U.P.S. shipping _$2.00_

Total enclosed _____

Name _____

Address _____

City _____ State _____ ZIP _____